THE PROPHETIC IMAGINATION

Praise for *The Prophetic Imagination*, 40th Anniversary Edition

"Years ago, as I struggled to envision a ministry that would engage both the prophetic and the pastoral, Walter Brueggemann's *The Prophetic Imagination* gave the world a fresh vision of the role of imagination in the inevitable confrontation between what Howard Thurman terms 'the religion of Jesus' and what Brueggemann calls 'the royal consciousness.' In the years since that revelation, yesterday's dilemmas birthed today's crises, which now loom as tomorrow's catastrophes. Even amid these shadows, Brueggemann still emboldens us to endure and even to overcome these troubles, not merely by the tenacity of blues lamentation and the transcendence of gospel communion, but also by prophetic improvisations that jazz the song of Joshua and crumble the walls thrown up by the politics of domination."

— WILLIAM J. BARBER II,
author of *The Third Reconstruction*

"Few authors have influenced my spiritual formation more than Walter Brueggemann, and few books more than *The Prophetic Imagination*. Brueggemann is one of the greatest theologians we have alive today. If you have not read this book, please do. If you have read it before, read it again. *The Prophetic Imagination* is precisely what the church needs right now."

— SHANE CLAIBORNE, activist and author of *Executing Grace* and *Red Letter Revolution*

"When I first read *The Prophetic Imagination* in college, it changed my life. Now, forty years after its initial publication, Brueggemann's book remains as timely as ever, retaining all of its power, insight, and daring. This anniversary edition—beautifully introduced by Davis Hankins—ensures that this classic work is available to inspire another generation to resist the static triumphalism of Pharaoh (in countless contemporary incarnations), to criticize the dominant totalizing consciousness, and to energize the people of God in the face of profound grief."

— Brent A. Strawn, Emory University

"Walter Brueggemann's *The Prophetic Imagination* has drawn many a student, seminarian, preacher, and more than a few laypeople on the strength of the title alone, resonant with much of black preaching where the 'sanctified imagination' is regularly engaged. This text has guided generations of biblical interpreters to take the prophetic encounter and vocation as more than protest or religiopolitical disagreement in and beyond the text. The book remains relevant—eminently readable and teachable."

— Wil Gafney, Brite Divinity School

"At a time when tradition seems to have become the property of the status quo, this book is more relevant than ever. As tradition shifts sides, it becomes subversive of the dominant religious, political, and economic developments, and so new energies are set free that push toward liberation. While this has been going on for thousands of years, the increasing challenges of the past forty years since this book was written—threatening to destroy both humanity and the planet—underscore its ongoing importance."

— JOERG RIEGER, Vanderbilt University

"Essential reading for generations of scholars and pastors, *The Prophetic Imagination* has been catalytic for those yearning to understand biblical prophecy and strengthen their own prophetic witness. Over against the hopelessness generated by repressive ideology, Brueggemann insists that we can choose as the prophets did: neither denial nor acquiescence, but visionary resistance. Brueggemann presses a brilliant case for prophetic imagination as the only choice that will not leave us co-opted by the relentless manipulations of empire."

— CAROLYN J. SHARP, Yale Divinity School

"Walter Brueggemann's *The Prophetic Imagination* is timeless; yet, at the same time, it feels as if he wrote it 'for such a time as this.' The convicting yet hopeful voice of Brueggemann is much like the prophets he writes of from the Hebrew Bible—indeed, he is the conscience of our time."

— CYNTHIA SHAFER-ELLIOTT,
William Jessup University

"*The Prophetic Imagination* opened our eyes and ears to the power and purposiveness of the prophets' vision. Practicing prophetic imagination is no less urgent a vocation today, in the face of the omnipresent calculus of human expendability. That this slender book seems both as inspiring and as unerringly realistic today as forty years ago is testament that Walter Brueggemann has described that vocation with precision; this new edition frames his argument as a word on target for a time that critically needs it."

— NEIL ELLIOTT, author of *Liberating Paul*
and *The Arrogance of Nations*

Reims Portail nord, ébrasement droit. Jérémie (?) 1210. Repros interd. Cliché Giraudon

THE PROPHETIC IMAGINATION

40th Anniversary Edition

WALTER BRUEGGEMANN

Foreword by Davis Hankins

FORTRESS PRESS
Minneapolis

For sisters in ministry
who teach me daily about
the power of grief
and
the gift of amazement

Contents

Foreword

The bibliography of works by Walter Brueggemann is astounding, surely unparalleled among his peers. He has published at a dizzying pace on a vast array of subjects in multiple genres, including works of critical scholarship, reviews, sermons, poetic prayers, and more. That so much of Brueggemann's variegated and sprawling corpus is already anticipated in this slim book is therefore astonishing. In his "Preface to the Revised Edition" (2001), Brueggemann declares that this book was his "first publication in which I more-or-less found my own voice." At the risk of oversimplification, I think that the argument that he voices here involves a few clear steps.

Brueggemann approaches exploitative societies as sustained by various ideologies. Such ideologies silence any actual or imagined threats to the reigning inequities that consolidate wealth and power for the benefit of a few to the exclusion of others. The prophetic task begins with grief that names the realities within such a social situation of pain, loss, fear, resentment, and antagonism. Such mourning enables a community to break through the denial, numbness, and inhumanity of exploitation. As the prophetic cry loosens the grip of dominant ideologies, it also energizes and empowers a community out of indifference into action. Now engaged, hope becomes possible not only for healing but also for an alternative mode of life, which prophets must articulate and enact with artistry potent enough to resist domestication. Prophetic imagination proceeds through these three basic steps: (1) it refuses denial and penetrates despair with honest cries over pain and loss that result from social injustices; (2) it overcomes amnesia by drawing on ancient, artistic traditions that energize the community to imagine and live into a more just order; and (3) it ends in hope and gratitude for the surprising gift of an emancipated future. These steps have remained paradigmatic in Brueggemann's subsequent work to an extent that, while it may appear that Brueggemann has written scores of books, one might also suggest that he has never stopped writing *The Prophetic Imagination*.

I believe there are two main reasons why *The Prophetic Imagination* has needed four decades of ongoing, still unfinished development. First, the approach to the biblical materials that it adopts is so broad, rich, provocative, and unlike most biblical scholarship that some of its deepest insights needed further intellectual development in order to be fully appreciated. This is not simply a matter of Brueggemann being ahead of his time, although I think that he was; it also seems true that this book was ahead of its author. Brueggemann admits in the preface to the 2001 edition that the title's conjunction of "prophetic" and "imagination" was a late decision that "was entirely happenstance." Subsequently, Brueggemann's significant publications on the pivotal and various roles that imagination plays—in biblical texts, their interpretation, and in communal practices—make it nearly impossible to view the title as a fortuitous happenstance.[1] That is, the title's precise formulation now seems absolutely necessary because we have since learned that no prophetic text or task can be grasped without considering the function of imagination. This point now appears clearly within *The Prophetic Imagination*, yet it could not have been as clear to its initial readers.

The gift of forty years of hindsight and the ongoing work of many scholars, including Brueggemann, have cast into fine relief the depth and richness of the claims in this book. Brueggemann's work on the imagination, for example, participates in larger developments in literary criticism, philosophy, and other fields. Sometimes designated poststructuralism or postmodernism, these developments refer in part to an increasing appreciation for the role of nonconceptual content—such as performance, way of life, enactment, images, and other imaginary features—in the production of conceptual content and the assessment of its value. Rather than continuing to pursue this point in relation to theory, however, I can offer a different, more concrete example from my personal experience.

In a seminar that I teach on prophetic rhetoric and literature, I typically assign *The Prophetic Imagination* after students read Kathleen O'Connor's 2011 monograph on the book of Jeremiah.[2] O'Connor and Brueggemann enjoyed a long and happy time as colleagues at Columbia Theological Seminary, where I had the good fortune of being their student. Their relationship proved to be, over time, one of mutual support, stimulation, and evocation. O'Connor approaches Jeremiah in a way that is explicitly indebted to Brueggemann's work, but she adds a thorough engagement with trauma and disaster studies. The latter field of inquiry emerged as a robust and distinct area of scholarship only in the last decade of the twentieth century, so it is astonishing that Brueggemann's reflections on grief and mourning in this book (first published in 1978) align so extensively with recent research. One might reasonably read *The Prophetic Imagination* first, and then O'Connor, since she engages his book and supplements it with attention to a new field of inquiry. But in my experience, more is learned by reading O'Connor first because her presentation of the theoretical work and practical experiences gained by those who study and treat the effects of trauma and disaster provide a background against which the depth and implications of Brueggemann's claims can be better appreciated. For example, Brueggemann attends to the numbness, denial, and the powerful deadening hold by which the dominant, royal consciousness perpetuates its status quo. Students are more prepared to understand this social reality *after* they have considered how these same symptoms manifest in, for example, the psychological responses that typically appear and function as coping mechanisms in victims of domestic abuse. And Brueggemann's description of the positive social and political potential of narrating painful experiences and expressing grief is even clearer *after* reading about the essential role that they play in therapeutic treatment.

The second reason why I think that *The Prophetic Imagination* has required four decades of ongoing articulation is because the problematic features that this book diagnoses in the social situation have not faded into the past, and because the prophetic program of criticizing and energizing that the book advocates retains similar relevance and vitality. First, among the many factors that differentiate what Brueggemann calls the royal situation from the prophetic imagination, the unequal distribution of wealth and economic practices of unjust extraction play a pivotal role in the social inequities and oppression that characterize the former and summon the latter. Beginning in the late 1970s, and certainly by the 2001 revision of *The Prophetic Imagination*, inequalities in wealth and income, which had been relatively low and stable for three decades after World War II, began to increase dramatically in the rich countries of Europe and especially the United States.[3] Over the course of this meteoric rise in income and wealth inequalities, wages for the majority of the population in the United States have remained stagnant.[4] Systemic forces that have exacerbated disparities in wealth and income sustain this status quo. For Brueggemann, "prophetic ministry has to do not primarily with addressing specific public crises but with addressing, in season and out of season, the dominant crisis that is enduring and resilient, of having our alternative vocation co-opted and domesticated" (p. 3). From an economic perspective, this means that prophets primarily need to address not this or that overpaid CEO, super-manager, university chancellor, college football coach, or professional athlete, but the dominant social and economic forces that drive steadily increasing divergences in wealth distribution. Similarly, the question is not whether our economic system has enabled growth and benefited lives, but whether we can imagine an alternative kind of economy that might foster broader benefits for far more people in the future.

Such economic realities cannot be separated from politics and public policy. Many policy decisions over the last four decades have played a major role in these increased inequalities, such as those that have contributed to the emerging dominance of finance within our economic system—even in the decade since 2008 when finance played such a pivotal role in nearly collapsing the global economy.[5] Other political tensions have similarly persisted. Brueggemann consistently shows how royal orders desperately try to maintain power and control in various ways, such as phony claims to moral supremacy, just retribution, peace, and well-being, in order to avoid critique and mask realities of self-interest, victim-blaming, and inequality.

The prophet should mourn and criticize actions that enable the persistence of situations that compromise core values and imagine alternative policies that define national interests on the basis of those values. This is, in fact, how Martin Luther King began his "Dream" speech. He urged America to honor the "promissory note" that the Constitution and the Declaration of Independence offered African Americans, which they had not yet been able to cash.[6] Prophets characteristically summon their communities to turn from their current failings so as to be true to their most fundamental values.

Race has continued to be a contemporary issue over the decades since *The Prophetic Imagination* first appeared, as has the struggle for gender equality and rights, as well as questions about immigrants, refugees, foreigners, and more. Brueggemann dedicated this book to "sisters in ministry," and now *Time* magazine has named #MeToo the 2017 "person of the year." It is also noteworthy that the last time I taught the course mentioned above on prophecy, students were astonished that Stokely Carmichael was not part of Black Lives Matter but instead spoke with such contemporaneity over forty years ago. This is not to deny progress on these issues in the United States, for prophetic leaders like Carmichael have not worked and died in vain. But the underlying root of these social problems remains, along with the steps that can be taken toward an alternative. As William Barber regularly mentions in his Moral Mondays movement and in his renewed Poor People's Campaign, *The Prophetic Imagination* helps to identify and articulate the problem, and to imagine and pursue a more emancipatory future, which is why Brueggemann's book has needed forty years of ongoing implementation.

The Prophetic Imagination never treats biblical texts as mere vehicles for policy positions or cultural critique. Brueggemann emphasizes throughout the importance and the implications of the fact that the prophets were not pundits but poets and preachers. Just as the prophets articulate a poetic idiom that frees imaginations from the flat prose of a dominant discourse that admits nothing unexpected, so too does the prophets' Lord operate with agency in an arena that is unacknowledged and even unknown to the prevailing consciousness. This God is not defined by doctrines or wedded to social institutions but regularly surprises the human community with new meanings, unforeseen possibilities, and unconscious truths that the prophets voice in God's name. *The Prophetic Imagination* is one such instance; ultimately, it is an attempt to create a new future for Christianity as host for divine possibilities in a cultural context that is dominated by unacknowledged anxiety that issues in anti-neighborly resentment, aggression, and worse. Of course, mainstream Christianity has often, unfortunately, contributed to that toxic context, but Brueggemann's wager is that the prophetic tradition is like a foreign body within that toxicity—inside the church and out—that is capable of eroding it and constructing an alternative. Forty years after its initial publication in 1978, the need is no less urgent, and the promise of this book sounds even more compelling. The work that lies ahead is to imagine and enact that alternative. For that we can be grateful— and amazed!

> Davis Hankins
> Appalachian State University
> Martin Luther King Jr. Day 2018

Thanks to Brent A. Strawn for reading and commenting on an earlier draft of this foreword.

A Note about the 40th Anniversary Edition

Fortress Press is pleased to publish this new edition of *The Prophetic Imagination* to honor its fortieth year in print and to celebrate the legacy of Walter Brueggemann's many publishing projects with Fortress Press, twenty-eight volumes and counting! We are grateful for this long and enduring relationship, and we are honored to have been one of many conduits for Walter's voice.

Based on the revised edition published in 2001, this volume includes a new foreword by Davis Hankins and Walter Brueggemann's own "In Retrospect (PI at Forty)." We have updated the cover as a reminder that this groundbreaking volume is ever new and timely, calling forth fresh prophetic imagination in each generation.

Preface to the Second (Revised) Edition

The publication of *The Prophetic Imagination* in 1978 was my first publication in which I more-or-less found my own voice as a teacher in the church. Much has changed for me since then, but the basic thesis that I articulated there holds for me and continues to frame my ongoing work. There are indeed definitive continuities between what I said then and what I would say now.

I

At the same time, a great deal has changed since then. I mark three such changes. First, the changes in method and approach in the critical study of the Bible since then are immense. In 1978 or in the years just preceding when I wrote, scripture study was completely defined by historical criticism, even though the first hints of new approaches were on the horizon. For the study of the prophetic texts, this commitment to historical criticism meant understanding the prophetic personalities in their presumed historical contexts and then extrapolating from that text-in-context to general thematics. Derivatively, the practical use of prophetic texts in "prophetic ministry" meant rather regularly direct, confrontational encounter with established power in the way Amos seemed to confront Amaziah (Amos 7:10-17). Such an approach that, in

retrospect, seems somewhat simplistic did indeed fund and authorize bold and courageous ministries.

At that time, however, scripture study generally awaited the
articulation of methods that moved beyond or underneath historical criticism of a conventional kind. Specifically, social-scientific
criticism, stunningly introduced into Old Testament studies by
Norman Gottwald in 1979—the year after my book—opened the
way to see texts as ideological statements evoked by and evoking
specific forms of social action and policy, social authorization, and
social criticism.[1] Robert Wilson helped us to see that the prophets
are not lonely voices against the establishment but are in fact representative voices that give social expression to what may be important and engaged social constituencies.[2] The effect of such
study is to situate prophetic texts more densely in the interplay of
social forces that are in conflict over the correct characterization of
social reality. Thus the texts are brought more closely into contact
with the social processes in which they are imbedded and to which
the texts themselves may have contributed.

In like manner, critical study of the Old Testament in 1978 still
awaited the emergence of rhetorical criticism and its appreciation
of the generative, constitutive power of imagination. In 1978, the
same year as my book, Phyllis Trible published *God and the Rhetoric of Sexuality,* a definitive starting point in Old Testament study
for the ways in which public speech (and thus text) generate alternative worlds.[3] Partly out of rhetorical criticism and partly out of
the crucial work of Paul Ricoeur on imagination, it became generally evident that texts—in particular biblical texts—are acts of
imagination that offer and purpose "alternative worlds" that exist
because of and in the act of utterance.[4] Since that early publication
of Trible, there has been an explosion of literature on theological
imagination with the recognition, against dominant classical
views, that imagination is indeed a legitimate way of knowing.[5]
One consequence of this new awareness is that biblical texts, in
particular prophetic texts, could be seen as poetic scenarios of alternative social reality that might lead to direct confrontation with

"presumed, taken-for-granted worlds" (the old liberal assumption). The canonical text, as norm for an intergenerational community, might also serve to nurture and fund obedience that is not necessarily confrontational but that simply acts out of a differently perceived, differently received, differently practiced world (imagination/obedience). Thus a focus on rhetoric as generative imagination has permitted prophetic texts to be heard and reuttered as offers of reality counter to dominant reality that characteristically enjoys institutional, hegemonic authority but is characteristically uncritical of itself.

The second change since 1978 that I note is my own changed perspective. My dedication of that book to "sisters in ministry" plus my citation of José Porfirio Miranda on page 89 indicate that at that time I was only beginning (as most of us were only beginning) to integrate into my interpretive practice the perspectives that are associated with various forms of liberation theology. My continued attention to issues of a liberation hermeneutic has since that time intensified for me. The recurring critiques of liberation hermeneutics are of course well known; in general, however, those critiques strike me as misinformed and offered by critics who have the luxury of social distance from the sharp wounds of social reality. When one considers the issues of liberation and exploitation on the ground, then the intimate contact between biblical texts of a prophetic sort and matters of social justice, social interest, and social criticism seem to me to be incontrovertible. Moreover, the enmeshment of the United States church in the raging force of globalization and the easy accommodation of church faith and practice to consumer commoditism make the urgency of "prophetic consciousness" palpable among us, any critique of method to the contrary. In any case, I believe that the lines of argument I have laid out are, if anything, more important than at the time of my writing, precisely because the hegemonic power of the "royal consciousness" is all but totalizing among us. Thus my own conviction about the matter is intensified as I ponder my own faith in the context where I find myself called.

The third change that I identify is that the church community in its "mainline" expressions is increasingly decentered and disenfranchised since the time of my writing. There is much speculation and gnashing of teeth about the causes of such marginalization, and lots of culprits have been identified. But the likely "explanation" is the long-term and deep force of secularization. Whatever may be the cause of such marginalization of the church as an institution, the effect can hardly be doubted. The consequence of this social reality that concerns us is that the old confrontational model of "prophet versus established power," which was a replication of the Old Testament notion of "prophet versus king," is increasingly difficult to bring off and without great social effect. A confrontational model assumes that the "prophetic voice" has enough clout, either social or moral, to gain a hearing. Currently, the old "prophetic stance" of such churches lacks much of that authority, so that the old confrontational approach is largely ineffectual posturing. Given that social reality, which I think cannot be doubted, I suspect that whatever is "prophetic" must be more cunning and more nuanced and perhaps more ironic.

For that reason it is important to see that the prophetic texts that feature the great confrontations are not to be directly replicated and reenacted. Rather, they are to be seen as materials that might fund the would-be prophetic voice, to give wisdom and courage, but which then invite immense imagination to know how to move from such texts to actual circumstance. This move, required by contemporary context, is to take the prophetic texts as text and not as "personality," the tendency of the older confrontational model. Thus my accent on imagination has turned out to be exactly correct, for what is now required is that a relatively powerless prophetic voice must find imaginative ways that are rooted in the text but that freely and daringly move from the text toward concrete circumstance. Seen in that contextual way, "prophetic imagination" requires more than the old liberal confrontation if the point is not posturing but effecting change in social perspective and social policy.

II

Since I have suggested something of an equation of "royal consciousness" and "false consciousness," I should acknowledge one ongoing critique of my position by my friend J. J. M. Roberts and his students. The persistent judgment of that perspective is that I have been much too severe on the monarchy in the Old Testament and have treated the thematic of the royal too harshly and dismissively. Perhaps so. But I think it important to identify two grounds for the quite different nuance we each bring to the question. First, I have tried to do serious social criticism of the ideology that exists in the royal texts. That is, I have brought to the text my own hermeneutic of suspicion. I believe that is in order when one considers the outcome of the Solomonic reign that is terminated in the interplay of *idolatry* (1 Kgs 11:1-13) and *a critique of economic policy with reference to labor* (1 Kgs 12:1-19). The combination of idolatry and economic policy are telling in a suspicion about the monarchy expressed in the text. Second, it is evident that the monarchy was terminated and any reading of the Old Testament makes clear the sustained judgment that the termination is because of Torah disobedience. One can hardly, in my judgment, fail to see Torah disobedience apart from the realities of social practice. Thus I believe that any robust theological defense of the monarchy in the Old Testament as it was practiced on the ground must disregard any social analysis and must proceed in a kind of innocence. Third, I believe that the impetus for the defense of the monarchy is in order to be in a position to appreciate the coming of Christ as the fulfillment of the royal line. That is, I believe that the defense has a theological motivation, one that I think is remote from the kind of analysis I am doing. I do not intend to impute to my critics anything less than a legitimate scholarly judgment, and in the end it may be that we simply disagree on what the texts say. I imagine that none of our judgments is objective or disinterested, mine or theirs. I hope it is fair to try to state what I think the disagreement is about and regard my own judgment on the matter as a quite provisional one.

III

The interface of "prophetic" and "imagination" has turned out to be a most important one. I must admit, however, that the phrasing for the book was entirely happenstance, a title decision made late in the publication process. It is, nonetheless, a fortuitous one because prophetic faith in a flat, confrontational mode, without imagination, is a non-starter. Concerning the phrase of the title, I am delighted to notice that in 1982, just after my book was published, F. Asals offered his study of the work of Flannery O'Connor in his book *Flannery O'Connor: The Imagination of Extremity.*[6] Even better than that, his sixth chapter is titled "The Prophetic Imagination."[7] It is of course too much to associate my writing, then or now, with the savage artistry of Flannery O'Connor. I am sure, nonetheless, that the joining of "prophetic" to "imagination" leads inescapably in an artistic direction in which truth is told in a way and at an angle that assures it will not be readily coopted or domesticated by hegemonic interpretive power. Of O'Connor's work, Asals judges:

> The imagination, O'Connor discovered, might accomplish much more; it might become the channel of visionary awareness. . . . For O'Connor, as for Aquinas, it is the imagination, with its roots deep in the human unconscious, that is the link between the depths of the self and the unseen reaches of the universe, that can reveal to finite man his apocalyptic destiny . . . the imagination for her is as dangerous a force as any named by Freud, for what it opens to, in those shattering climaxes when it achieves release, are the unwanted visions that ravage the lives of her protagonists.[8]
>
>   . . . as the institutional guardian of the prophetic Word, the church has hardly been hospitable to the individual voice crying, "Thus sayeth the Lord."[9]
>
>   . . . Far from denying the body and the senses, the asceticism in the later fiction works consistently to affirm them, to release them from the false consciousness of her protagonists in order to experience reality. But reality, to the prophetic mind, is always double:

"This world, no more shadow of ideas in an upper sphere, is real, but not absolute; the world's reality is contingent upon compatibility with God."[10] For O'Connor's sacramentalism, it is the natural world that becomes the vehicle for the supernatural, and her characters' literal return to their senses becomes the means of opening their imaginations to receive it.[11]

Suffering is central to the prophetic consciousness. "The prophet is prepared for pain. One of the effects of his presence is to intensify the people's capacity for suffering, to rend the veil that lies between life and pain."[12] . . . This ascetic imperative in O'Connor is a part of that prophetic consciousness. . . .[13]

As a writer of fiction, Flannery O'Connor simply had no interest in—no imagination for—"a socially desirable Christianity."[14]

Concrete, passionate, and imaginative, prophetic in its form, prophetic speech is nonetheless "a sharp sword," conveying a vision "designed to shock rather than edify."[15]

Moderation is a delusion, and only extremists are in touch with reality.[16]

As O'Connor's writing is dense, so the allusions in Asals's analysis are dense, and I will not unpack them here. It is sufficient to notice, first, that O'Connor appeals a great deal to Abraham Heschel, also definingly important for my work. Second, it is important to notice that her notion of the prophetic is truth that is inexplicable and out beyond the normalcy of her characters. Thus, I submit, *prophetic* must be *imaginative* because it is urgently out beyond the ordinary and the reasonable.

The analysis of Asals makes clear that O'Connor stresses a concern for "false consciousness" that I have termed "royal consciousness," the defining power of suffering for the reception of truth, that established institutions and social conventions are deeply inhospitable to such imagination. It is inescapable that prophetic utterance and action turn out to be absurd, but it is an absurdity that may be the very truth of obedient imagination.

IV

Because this book intends to serve the practice of the church, I take the liberty of commenting on "the natural habitat" of prophetic voices. Evidently God can "raise up prophets" and authorize prophetic voices and deeds in the fullness of God's own freedom, anywhere, anytime, in any circumstance. If, however, we are to think from the human side of the matter, it will not surprise that some social environments are more hospitable than others to prophets and more likely to be the locus of their emergence. I take it, following Wilson's notion of "peripheral prophets," that prophets are "naturally" in subcommunities that stand in tension with the dominant community in any political economy.[17]

The subcommunity that may generate prophecy will participate in the public life of the dominant community; it does so, however, from a certain perspective and with a certain intention. Such a subcommunity is likely to be one in which

* there is a *long and available memory* that sinks the present generation deep into an identifiable past that is available in song and story;

* there is an available, expressed *sense of pain* that is owned and recited as a real social fact, that is visibly acknowledged in a public way, and that is understood as unbearable for the long term;

* there is an *active practice of hope,* a community that knows about promises yet to be kept, promises that stand in judgment on the present;

* there is an *effective mode of discourse* that is cherished across the generations, that is taken as distinctive, and that is richly coded in ways that only insiders can know.

In short, such a subcommunity is one in which the first-line, elemental realities of human, bodily, historical existence are appreciated, honored, and treasured. It is obvious that such a subcommunity knows itself to be positioned for the long-term in tension with the dominant community that responds to the subcommunity at best as an inconvenience, at worst as an unbearable interruption.

From this characterization, three specific comments follow:

1. It is not surprising that the noteworthy "prophetic figures" of the twentieth century have emerged in oppressive situations not completely closed down by usurpatious technology, in circumstances wherein subcommunities could claim for themselves enough space in which to practice resistance and alternative.

2. The immense technological power of the United States makes the formation and maintenance of subcommunities of resistance and alternative in the United States exceedingly difficult. Moreover, for all of our treasured talk of "individual freedom," the force of homogeneity is immense—partly seductive, partly coercive, partly the irresistible effect of affluence, in any case not hospitable to "difference."

3. While a Christian congregation in the prosperous United States is not at all parallel to subcommunities of resistance and alternative in more manifestly brutal societies, the church as a subcommunity in the United States is a thinkable mode of ministry. This is not a championing of sectarian withdrawal—a charge often made against Stanley Hauerwas and Will Willimon—nor a cranky community of endless protest, dissent, and confrontive "social action." Rather, it is a suggestion about a community of peculiar discourse with practices of memory, hope, and pain that keep healthy human life available in the face of all the "virtual reality" now on offer in dominant culture. Reflection on biblical faith will indicate that the discourse of the biblical text provides ways of speech that make such a community possible. The formation and sustenance of such a subcommunity require a shared willingness to engage in gestures of resistance and acts of deep hope. These gestures and acts in turn require pastoral leadership that proceeds with an intentional ecclesial focus, namely, a subcommunity with an evangelical will for public engagement.

In our contemporary world we are able to notice prophets-in-the-face-of-oppression. It is not so easy in our electronic environment of consumerism to imagine prophetic discourse and prophetic action, but such consumerism is nonetheless likely the foremost circumstance of prophetic faith in the United States. As every vibrant subcommunity knows, the defining prerequisite for such a subcommunity is a conviction that it can and will be different because of the purposes of God that will not relent. A deficit in that conviction, to which to we are all prone, will produce despairing conformity, an atmosphere making the prophetic profoundly unlikely.

V

I was led into a wholly new understanding of theological imagination by the deeply unsettling and deeply reassuring book of William T. Cavanaugh, *Torture and Eucharist: Theology, Politics, and the Body of Christ.*[18] The book is an amazing critical reflection upon the role and conduct of the Roman Catholic Church in Chile during the years of terror under Pinochet. Cavanaugh's analysis of the intentionality of Pinochet's torture and terror is that it was designed to make human community impossible, to eliminate any chance of human dissent or human alternative, and so to assure the absolutism of the state.

In his analysis, Cavanaugh concludes that during the first, early years of that brutality, the church and its leadership were asleep at the switch and passively conceded everything to the regime. After a certain point, however, the bishops of the church began to realize that the community-forming miracle of the Eucharist was a vehicle for the rule of God and a practical instrument for generating communities of resistance against the state. Thus, on deep theological grounds as well as practical considerations, the Eucharist proved to be an effective, even if risky, antidote to torture.

In the final passages of his exposition, Cavanaugh reflects on the force of liturgic imagination by an appeal to the novel of Lawrence Thornton, *Imagining Argentina.*[19] In the novel, the key character, Carlos Rueda, is visited with "a peculiar miraculous gift," the capacity to create futures by acts of anticipatory imagination. Cavanaugh summarizes:

What is especially astonishing is that Carlos's gift is more than just the gift of seeing; his stories about people can actually alter reality. Men appear in the middle of the night to give back babies snatched with their mothers. Holes open in solid concrete walls, and tortured prisoners walk through to freedom. Carlos's imagination actually finds people who have disappeared. . . . Confronted with evidence of the miraculous, Carlos's friends nevertheless remain skeptical, convinced that Carlos cannot confront tanks with stories, helicopters with mere imagination. They can only see the conflict in terms of fantasy versus reality. Carlos, on the other hand, rightly grasps that the contest is not between imagination and the real, but between two types of imagination, that of the generals and that of their opponents. The nightmare world of torture and disappearance of bodies is inseparable from the generals' imagination of what Argentina and Argentines are. Carlos realizes that "he was being dreamed by [General] Gusman and the others, that he had been living inside their imagination."[20]

Cavanaugh then quotes from the novel itself:

They remember a time before the regime, but they do not take their imaginations beyond memory because hoping is too painful. So long as we accept what the men in the car imagine, we're finished. . . . We have to believe in the power of imagination because it is all we have, and ours is stronger than theirs.[21]

Cavanaugh then concludes in a reflection on the novel:

To refer to torture as the "imagination of the state" as I have done is obviously not to deny the reality of torture, but to call attention to the fact that torture is part of a drama of inscribing bodies to perform certain roles in the imaginative project which is the nation-state. Likewise, in *Imagining Argentina,* Carlos's imagination is manifested in real effects; escaping the imagination of the state means that bodies go free. The imagination is defined as nothing less than "the magnificent cause of being." Thornton's novel provides us with a glimpse of what it means to make the odd claim that the Eucharist is the key to Christian resistance to torture. To participate in the Eucharist is to live inside God's imagination. It is to be caught up into what is really real, the body of Christ. As human persons, body and soul, are incorporated into the performance of Christ's *corpus verum,* they resist the state's ability to define what is real through the mechanism of torture.[22]

Hardly anything remains to be said about imagination as theological force.

Except to note that clearly the need for Eucharistic imagination in the United States is very different from the need for it in the abusive contexts that prevailed in Argentina and Chile. Indeed, the difference is so great that one might judge there is no transfer of the power of imagination from one context to the other. Whereas the South American societies suffer torture and physical abuse, the cultural situation in the United States, satiated by consumer goods and propelled by electronic technology, is one of narcoticized insensibility to human reality. It may be, however, that torture and consumer satiation perform the same negative function: to deny a lively, communal imagination that resists a mindless humanity of despairing conformity.

If Eucharist is potentially an act of resistance and alternative to torture, perhaps Eucharistic imagination can also be a potential resistance and alternative to commodity satiation. It is evident that in our American society, as in those brutal contexts, there are two types of imagination, that of "the generals and their opponents," or that of consumer ideology and its resisters. The fact is that we in American society too easily live "inside this imagination" when prophetic imagination is capable of enabling us to live inside "God's imagination." Clearly, human transformative activity depends upon a transformed imagination. Numbness does not hurt like torture, but in a quite parallel way, numbness robs us of our capability for humanity.

What the prophetic tradition knows is that it could be different, and the difference can be enacted. At the end of this edition of the book I have listed examples of enacted prophetic imagination. Those listed there are persons, communities, and institutions that have refused to live inside an alien, numbing imagination and have embraced the very "imagination of God." The capacity of such alternative imagination is neither strong nor wise. But clearly,

> God's foolishness is wiser than human wisdom, and God's weakness is stronger than human strength. Consider your own call, brothers and sisters; not many of you were wise by human standards, not many were powerful, not many were of noble birth. But God chose what is foolish in the world to shame the wise; God chose what is weak in the world to shame the strong; God chose what is low and despised in the world, things that are not, to reduce to nothing the things that are (1 Cor 1:25-28).

VI

It remains for me to express thanks in connection with this second edition of the book. The impetus for the second edition has come from K. C. Hanson of Fortress Press. Beyond the impetus, Hanson has done the major part of the work in preparing the new edition. He has done extensive work on updating the body of the text, supplying new notes, and preparing the bibliographies at the end of the new version. Without him I would not have gotten this second rendering completed, and so I am deeply grateful to him.

In addition, I am as usual grateful to Tempie Alexander, who has done her usual careful and discerning work. I suppose it is fair as well to acknowledge the decades of readers who have read, used, and responded to this book, as well as kept it in circulation. I have the sense, along with the readers, of being engaged with life-or-death questions of mission that must now occupy us.

Walter Brueggemann
Pentecost season, 2000

Preface to the First Edition

The time may be ripe in the church for serious consideration of prophecy as a crucial element in ministry. To be sure, the student indignation of the sixties is all but gone, but there is at the same time a sobering and a return to the most basic issues of biblical faith.

The following discussion is an attempt to understand what the prophets were up to, if we can be freed from our usual stereotypes of foretellers or social protesters. Here it is argued that they were concerned with most elemental changes in human society and that they understood a great deal about how change is effected. The prophets understood the possibility of change as linked to emotional extremities of life. They understood the strange incongruence between public conviction and personal yearning. Most of all, they understood the distinctive power of language, the capacity to speak in ways that evoke newness "fresh from the word." It is argued here that a prophetic understanding of reality is based in the notion that all social reality does spring fresh from the word. It is the aim of every totalitarian effort to stop the language of newness, and we are now learning that where such language stops we find our humanness diminished.

These lectures were first presented to United Church of Christ and Disciples of Christ ministers in the state of Washington, where

I was generously hosted by Larry Pitman and James Halfaker, and at North Park Seminary, Chicago, where Dean Glenn Anderson was a source of encouragement and support. As in so many parts of my growth and learning, my colleague M. Douglas Meeks has stimulated these reflections.

This book is offered in thanksgiving for a growing number of my sisters who at long last are finding acceptance in ordained ministry. For me, of course, that distinguished group of colleagues is headed by my wife, Mary, who pastors in prophetic ways. It includes a growing number of women who have been my student colleagues at Eden Seminary.

I am growingly aware that this book is different because of the emerging feminine consciousness as it impacts our best theological thinking. That impacting is concerned not with abrasive crusading but with a different nuancing of all our perceptions. I do not think that women ministers and theologians are the first to have discerned the realities of grief and amazement in our lives, but they have helped us see them as important dimensions of prophetic reality. In many ways these sisters have permitted me to see what I otherwise might have missed. For that I am grateful—and amazed.

Walter Brueggemann
Eden Theological Seminary
Lent 1978

1

The Alternative Community
of Moses

A study of the prophets of Israel must try to take into account both
the evidence of the Old Testament and the contemporary situation
of the church. What we understand about the Old Testament must
be somehow connected with the realities of the church today. So I
shall begin with a statement of how I see our present situation and
the task facing us in ministry. I will not elaborate but only provide
a clue to the perspective from which I am presenting the subject.

The contemporary American church is so largely enculturated
to the American ethos of consumerism that it has little power to
believe or to act. This enculturation is in some way true across the
spectrum of church life, both liberal and conservative. It may not
be a new situation, but it is one that seems especially urgent and
pressing at the present time. That enculturation is true not only
of the institution of the church but also of us as persons. Our
consciousness has been claimed by false fields of perception and
idolatrous systems of language and rhetoric.

The internal cause of such enculturation is our loss of identity
through the abandonment of the faith tradition. Our consumer
culture is organized against history. There is a depreciation of
memory and a ridicule of hope, which means everything must be
held in the now, either an urgent now or an eternal now. Either
way, a community rooted in energizing memories and summoned
by radical hopes is a curiosity and a threat in such a culture. When

we suffer from amnesia, every form of serious authority for faith is in question, and we live unauthorized lives of faith and practice unauthorized ministries.

The church will not have power to act or believe until it recovers its tradition of faith and permits that tradition to be the primal way out of enculturation. This is not a cry for traditionalism but rather a judgment that the church has no business more pressing than the reappropriation of its memory in its full power and authenticity. And that is true among liberals who are too chic to remember and conservatives who have overlaid the faith memory with all kinds of hedges that smack of scientism and Enlightenment.

It is the task of prophetic ministry to bring the claims of the tradition and the situation of enculturation into an effective interface. That is, the prophet is called to be a child of the tradition, one who has taken it seriously in the shaping of his or her own field of perception and system of language, who is so at home in that memory that the points of contact and incongruity with the situation of the church in culture can be discerned and articulated with proper urgency.[1] In what follows, I want to urge that there are precise models in Scripture for discerning prophetic ministry in this way.

A study of the prophets of Israel must also try to take into account both the best discernment of contemporary scholarship and what the tradition itself seems to tell us. The tradition and contemporary scholarship are likely to be in some kind of tension, and we must try to be attentive to that. The weariness and serenity of the churches just now make it a good time to study the prophets and get rid of tired misconceptions. The dominant conservative misconception, evident in manifold bumper stickers, is that the prophet is a fortune-teller, a predictor of things to come (mostly ominous), usually with specific reference to Jesus. While one would not want to deny totally those facets of the practice of prophecy, there tends to be a kind of reductionism that is mechanical and therefore untenable. While the prophets are in a way future-tellers, they are concerned with the future as it impinges upon the present. Conversely, liberals who abdicated and turned all futuring over to conservatives have settled for a focus on the present. Thus prophecy is alternatively reduced to righteous indignation and, in circles where I move, prophecy is mostly understood as social action. Indeed, such a liberal understanding of prophecy is an attractive and face-saving device for any excessive abrasiveness in the service of almost any cause. Perhaps our best effort would be to let the futuring of such conservatives and the present criticism of the liberals correct each other. But even that is less than might be claimed. I believe that neither convention adequately understands what is really at issue in the Israelite understanding of prophecy.

The hypothesis I will explore here is this: *The task of prophetic ministry is to nurture, nourish, and evoke a consciousness and perception alternative to the consciousness and perception of the dominant culture around us.*[2] Thus I suggest that prophetic ministry has to do not primarily with addressing specific public crises but with addressing, in season and out of season, the dominant crisis that is enduring and resilient, of having our alternative vocation co-opted and domesticated. It may be, of course, that this enduring crisis manifests itself in any given time around concrete issues, but it concerns the enduring crisis that runs from concrete issue to concrete issue. That point is particularly important to ad hoc liberals who run from issue to issue without discerning the enduring domestication of vision in all of them.

The alternative consciousness to be nurtured, on the one hand, serves to *criticize* in dismantling the dominant consciousness. To that extent, it attempts to do what the liberal tendency has done: engage in a rejection and delegitimizing of the present ordering of things. On the other hand, that alternative consciousness to be nurtured serves to *energize* persons and communities by its promise of another time and situation toward which the community of faith may move. To that extent, it attempts to do what the conservative tendency has done, to live in fervent anticipation of the newness that God has promised and will surely give.

In thinking this way, the key word is *alternative,* and every prophetic minister and prophetic community must engage in a struggle with that notion. Thus, alternative to what? In what ways alternative? How radically alternative? Finally, is there a thinkable alternative that will avoid domestication? And, quite concretely, how does one present and act out alternatives in a community of faith which on the whole does not understand that there are any alternatives or is not prepared to embrace such if they come along? Thus it is a practice of ministry for which there is little readiness; indeed, not even among its would-be practitioners. So my programmatic urging is that every act of a minister who would be prophetic is part of a way of evoking, forming, and reforming an alternative community. And this applies to every facet and every practice of ministry. It is a measure of our enculturation that the various acts of ministry (for example, counseling, administration, even liturgy) have taken on lives and functions of their own rather than being seen as elements of the one prophetic ministry of formation and reformation of alternative community.

The functional qualifiers, *critical* and *energizing*, are important. I suggest that the dominant culture, now and in every time, is grossly uncritical, cannot tolerate serious and fundamental criticism, and will go to great lengths to stop it. Conversely, the dominant culture is a wearied culture, nearly unable to be seriously energized to new promises from God. We know, of course, that none of us relishes criticism, but we may also recognize that none of us much relishes energizing either, for that would demand something of us. The task of prophetic ministry is to hold together criticism and energizing, for I should urge that either by itself is not faithful to our best tradition. Our faith tradition understands that it is precisely the dialectic of criticizing and energizing that can let us be seriously faithful to God. And we may even suggest that to choose between criticizing and energizing is the temptation, respectively, of liberalism and conservativism. Liberals are good at criticism but often have no word of promise to speak; conservatives tend to future well and invite to alternative visions, but a germane criticism by the prophet is often not forthcoming. For those of us personally charged with this ministry, we may observe that to be called where this dialectic is maintained is an awesome call. And each of us is likely to fall to one side or the other.

As a beginning point in these considerations, I propose that our understanding of prophecy comes out of the covenantal tradition of Moses. I do not minimize the important scholarly contributions concerning non-Israelite antecedents to prophecy in Israel. These include (1) studies in the Canaanite phenomenon of ecstasy, surely echoed in 1 Samuel 10 and 19; and, more recently, (2) the evidence from Mari and Assyria concerning institutional offices of prophecy, both in the cult and in the court.[3] Both these kinds of evidence illuminate practices and conventions to which Israel undoubtedly appealed in its extensive borrowing. But the tradition itself is not ambiguous when it comes to the dominating figure of Moses who provides our primary understandings. That is to say, the shaping of Israel took place from inside its own experience and confession of faith and not through external appropriation from somewhere else. That urging is fundamental for this discussion, for I am urging in parallel fashion that if the church is to be faithful it must be formed and ordered from the inside of its experience and confession and not by borrowing from sources external to its own life.[4]

The ministry of Moses, as George Mendenhall and Norman Gottwald have most recently urged, represents a radical break with the social reality of Pharaoh's Egypt.[5] The newness and radical innovations of Moses and Israel in this period can hardly be over-stated. Most of us are probably so used to these narratives that we have become insensitive to the radical and revolutionary social reality that emerged because of Moses. It is clear that the emergence of Israel by the hand of Moses cannot be extrapolated from any earlier reality. Obviously nothing like the Kenite hypothesis (that Moses learned his monotheism from his father-in-law, Jethro the Kenite) or the monotheism of the eighteenth dynasty in Egypt (instituted by Pharaoh Akhenaton) will help us at all. While there are some hints that the God of Israel is known to be the God of the fathers (see. Exod 15:2), that evidence is at best obscure. In any case, the overriding experience of Exodus is decisive and not some memory now only hinted at in the tradition. However those antecedents are finally understood, *the appearance of a new social reality* is unprecedented. Israel in the thirteenth century is indeed ex nihilo. And that new social reality drives us to the category of revelation.[6] Israel can only be understood in terms of the new call of God and his assertion of an alternative social reality. Prophecy is born precisely in that moment when the emergence of social political reality is so radical and inexplicable that it has nothing less than a theological cause. Theological cause without social political reality is only of interest to a professional religionist, and social political reality without theological cause need not concern us here. But it is being driven by the one to the other that requires us to speak of and wonder about the call to the prophetic.[7]

Breaking with Triumphalism and Oppression

The radical break of Moses and Israel from imperial reality is a two-dimensioned break from both the religion of static triumphalism and the politics of oppression and exploitation. Moses dismantled the religion of static triumphalism by exposing the gods and showing that in fact they had no power and were not gods. Thus, the mythical legitimacy of Pharaoh's social world is destroyed, for it is shown that such a regime appeals to sanctions that in fact do not exist. The mythic claims of the empire are ended by the disclosure of *the alternative religion of the freedom of God.*[8] In place of the gods of Egypt, creatures of the imperial consciousness, Moses discloses that Yahweh, the sovereign one who acts in his lordly freedom, is extrapolated from no social reality and is captive to no social perception but acts from his own person toward his own purposes.

At the same time, Moses dismantles the politics of oppression and exploitation by countering it with a *politics of justice and compassion.* The reality emerging out of the Exodus is not just a new religion or a new religious idea or a vision of freedom but the emergence of a new social community in history, a community

that has historical body, that had to devise laws, patterns of gov-
ernance and order, norms of right and wrong, and sanctions of
accountability. The participants in the Exodus found themselves,
undoubtedly surprisingly to them, involved in the intentional
formation of a *new social community* to match the vision of *God's
freedom*. That new social reality, which is utterly discontinuous
with Egypt, lasted in its alternative way for 250 years. ← + then what?

We will not understand the meaning of prophetic imagination
unless we see the connection between the *religion of static triumphalism* and the *politics of oppression and exploitation*. Karl Marx had
discerned the connection when he observed that the criticism of
religion is the ultimate criticism and must lead to the criticism of
law, economics, and politics.[9] The gods of Egypt are the immov-
able lords of order. They call for, sanction, and legitimate a society
of order, which is precisely what Egypt had. In Egypt, as Frankfort
has show, there were no revolutions, no breaks for freedom. There
were only the necessary political and economic arrangements to
provide order, "naturally," the order of Pharaoh. Thus the religion
of the static gods is not and never could be disinterested, but inevitably it served the interests of the people in charge, presiding over
the order and benefiting from the order. And the functioning of
that society testified to the rightness of the religion because kings
did prosper and bricks did get made.

It is the marvel of prophetic faith that both imperial religion
and imperial politics could be broken. Religiously, the gods were
declared no-gods. Politically, the oppressiveness of the brickyard
was shown to be ineffective and not necessary to human community. Moses introduced not just the new free God and not just
a message of social liberation. Rather, his work came precisely at
the engagement of the *religion of God's freedom* with the *politics of
human justice*. Derivative from Marx, we can learn from these
traditions that finally we will not have a politics of justice and
compassion unless we have a religion of God's freedom. We are
indeed made in the image of some God. And perhaps we have
no more important theological investigation than to discern in

whose image we have been made. Our sociology is predictably derived from, legitimated by, and reflective of our theology. And if we gather around a static god of order who only guards the interests of the "haves," oppression cannot be far behind. Conversely, if a God is disclosed who is free to come and go, free from and even against the regime, free to hear and even answer slave cries, free from all proper godness as defined by the empire, then it will bear decisively upon sociology because the freedom of God will surface in the brickyards and manifest itself as justice and compassion.

My impression is that we have split those two items much too easily but not without reason. The liberal tendency has been to care about the politics of justice and compassion but to be largely uninterested in the freedom of God. Indeed, it has been hard for liberals to imagine that theology mattered, for all of that seemed irrelevant. And it was thought that the question of God could be safely left to others who still worried about such matters. As a result, social radicalism has been like a cut flower without nourishment, without any sanctions deeper than human courage and good intentions. Conversely, it has been the tendency in other quarters to care intensely about God, but uncritically, so that the God of well-being and good order is not understood to be precisely the source of social oppression. Indeed, a case can be made that unprophetic conservatives did not take God seriously enough to see that our discernment of God has remarkable sociological implications. And between liberals who imagine God to be irrelevant to sociology and conservatives who unwittingly use a notion of God for social reasons because they do not see how the two belong together, there is little to choose. Here it is enough to insist that Moses, paradigm for prophet, carried the alternative in both directions: a religion of God's freedom as alternative to the static imperial religion of order and triumph and a politics of justice and compassion as alternative to the imperial politics of oppression. The point that prophetic imagination must ponder is that there is no freedom

what is "God?
freedom?

of God without the politics of justice and compassion, and there is no politics of justice and compassion without a religion of the freedom of God.

The program of Moses is not the freeing of a little band of slaves as an escape from the empire, though that is important enough, especially if you happen to be in that little band. Rather, his work is nothing less than an assault on the consciousness of the empire, aimed at nothing less than the dismantling of the empire both in its social practices and in its mythic pretensions. Note the significance of Martin Luther King Jr.'s leadership in integrating a lunch counter or a local bus line! Israel emerged not by Moses' hand—although not without Moses' hand—as a genuine alternative community. The prophetic tradition knows that it bears a genuine alternative to a theology of God's enslavement and a sociology of human enslavement. That genuine alternative, entrusted to us who bear that calling, is rooted not in social theory or in righteous indignation or in altruism but in the genuine alternative that Yahweh is. Yahweh makes possible and requires an alternative theology and an alternative sociology. Prophecy begins in discerning how genuinely alternative he is.

Prophetic Criticism

The alternative consciousness wrought through Moses is characterized by criticizing and energizing. I will pursue this in more detail later, but these comments are in order now. The narrative of the Exodus is designed to show the radical criticism and radical delegitimizing of the Egyptian empire. At the beginning (Exod 5:7-10) the Egyptians are in full flower and full power. They "wheel and deal" and are subject to none:

> Let heavier work be laid upon the men that they may labor at it
> and pay no regard to lying words. So the taskmasters and the
> foremen of the people went out and said to the people, "Thus
> says Pharaoh."

Notice how the language is shaped to evoke anger and bring to expression the deep resentment at this whole system. But the story moves. At the end, these same masters, taskmasters, and foremen are vanquished, humiliated, and banished from history:

> The Egyptians whom you see today, you shall never see again. (14:13)
>
> Thus the LORD saved Israel that day from the hand of the Egyptians; and Israel saw the Egyptians dead upon the seashore. (14:30)

From beginning to end the narrative shows, with no rush to conclude, how the religious claims of Egyptian gods are nullified by this Lord of freedom. The narrative shows, with delighted lingering, how the politics of oppression is overcome by the practice of justice and compassion. And between the beginning and the end, the moment of dismantling is the plague cycle, a narrative that cannot be told too often, for it testifies to what cannot be explained, surely not the reason of the empire. It happens in this way: In the first two plagues, concerning the turn of the Nile and the frogs, the powerful work of Moses and Aaron is matched by Egyptian "research and development" people. Two plagues into the scene nothing is changed and the power of Egypt is not challenged. The empire knows how to play "anything you can do, I can do better." But then comes the third plague:

> Aaron stretched out his hand with his rod, and struck the dust of the earth, and there came gnats on man and beast; all the dust of the earth became gnats throughout all the land of Egypt. The magicians tried by their secret arts to bring forth gnats, but they could not! (Exod 8:17-18)

The Egyptian empire could not! The gods of Egypt could not! The scientists of the regime could not! The imperial religion was dead! The politics of oppression had failed! That is the ultimate criticism, that the assured and alleged power of the dominant culture is now shown to be fraudulent. Criticism is not carping and denouncing. It is asserting that false claims to authority and power cannot keep their promises, which they could not in the face of the free God. It is only a matter of time until they are dead on the seashore.   *who her?*

But the criticism has another dimension. Plastaras[10] has seen that the narrative of liberation begins with the grieving complaint of Israel:

> And the people of Israel groaned under their bondage, and cried out for help, and their cry under bondage came up to God. And God heard their groaning, and God remembered his covenant. . . . And God saw the people of Israel, and God knew their condition. (Exod 2:23-25)

I will urge later that the real criticism begins in the capacity to grieve because that is the most visceral announcement that things are not right. Only in the empire are we pressed and urged and invited to pretend that things are all right—either in the dean's office or in our marriage or in the hospital room. And as long as the empire can keep the pretense alive that things are all right, there will be no real grieving and no serious criticism.

But think what happens if the Exodus is the primal scream that permits the beginning of history.[11] In the verb "cry out" (*za'aq*) there is a bit of ambiguity because on the one hand it is a cry of misery and wretchedness with some self-pity, while it also functions for the official filing of a legal complaint. The mournful one is the plaintiff. As Erhard Gerstenberger has observed,[12] it is characteristic of Israel to complain rather than lament; that is, Israel does not voice resignation but instead expresses a militant sense of being wronged with the powerful expectation that it will be heard and answered. Thus the history of Israel begins on the day when its people no longer address the Egyptian gods who will not listen and cannot answer. The life of freedom and justice comes when they risk the freedom of the free God against the regime.

The grieving of Israel—perhaps self-pity and surely complaint but never resignation—is the beginning of criticism. It is made clear that things are not as they should be, not as they were promised, and not as they must be and will be. Bringing hurt to public expression is an important first step in the dismantling criticism that permits a new reality, theological and social, to emerge. That cry which begins history is acknowledged by Yahweh as history gathers power:

> I have seen the affliction of my people who are in Egypt, and have
> heard their cry because of their taskmasters; I know their suffer-
> ings, and I have come down to deliver them out of the hand of the
> Egyptians. (Exod 3:7-8)
> And now, behold, the cry of the people of Israel has come to me,
> and I have seen the oppression with which the Egyptians oppress
> them. Come, I will send you. (3:9-10)

That cry which is the primal criticism is articulated again in Exod 8:12. Moses and Aaron now know that serious intervention and intercession must be made to Yahweh the God of freedom and not to the no-gods of Egypt. In 5:8 and 15 there is still a cry to Pharaoh, still a looking to the empire for help and relief: "Therefore they cry, 'Let us go and offer sacrifice to our God.' . . . Then the foremen of the people of Israel came and cried to Pharaoh. . . ."

By the middle of the plague cycle Israel has disengaged from the empire, cries no more to it, expects nothing of it, acknowledges it in no way, knows it cannot keep its promises, and knows that nothing is either owed it or expected of it. That is the ultimate criticism which leads to dismantling.

In the narrative, criticism moves and builds. The grieving cry learns to turn away from false listeners and turn toward the one who can help. Prophetic criticism, as Dorothee Soelle has suggested,[13] consists in mobilizing people to their real restless grief and in nurturing them away from cry-hearers who are inept at listening and indifferent in response. Surely history consists primarily of speaking and being answered, crying and being heard. If that is true, it means there can be no history in the empire because the cries are never heard and the speaking is never answered. And if the task of prophecy is to empower people to engage in history, then it means evoking cries that expect answers, learning to address them where they will be taken seriously, and ceasing to look to the numbed and dull empire that never intended to answer in the first place.

Curiously, the criticism of cry is intensified as the narrative develops. In the report of Exod 11:6 and 12:30 the mighty empire cries out:

> And there shall be a great cry throughout all the land of Egypt as there has never been, nor ever shall be again. (11:6)
>
> And Pharaoh rose up in the night, he, and all his servants, and all the Egyptians; and there was a great cry in Egypt, for there was not a house where one was not dead. (12:30)

Both times the cry concerns the killing of the firstborn, even the firstborn of Pharaoh who was born to rule. That is highly ironic, for now the self-sufficient and impervious regime is reduced to the role of a helpless suppliant. The cry of Israel becomes an empowering cry; the cry of Egypt is one of dismantling helplessness. But it is too late. History has begun, and the initiative has been taken by the new God for the new community.

When did the plagues hit Egypt — (before) or after Exodus?

The empire is left to grieve over its days of not caring and its gods of order and its politics of injustice, which are all now ended. Criticism has reached its goal.

Prophetic Energizing

The alternative consciousness wrought by Moses also provides a model for energizing. Moses and this narrative create the sense of new realities that can be trusted and relied upon just when the old realities had left us hopeless. It is the task of the prophet to bring to expression the new realities against the more visible ones of the old order. Energizing is closely linked to hope. We are energized not by that which we already possess but by that which is promised and about to be given. It is the tendency of liberals to rail and polemicize, but in the lack of faith or bad faith of so many it is not believed that something is about to be given. Egypt was without energy precisely because it did not believe anything was promised and about to be given. Egypt, like every imperial and eternal now, believed everything was already given, contained, and possessed. If there is any point at which most of us are manifestly co-opted, it is in this way. We do not believe that there will be newness but only that there will be merely a moving of the pieces into new patterns.

It is precisely the prophet who speaks against such managed data and who can energize toward futures that are genuinely new and not derived. I suggest three energizing dimensions to this narrative that are important for prophetic imagination.

First, energy comes from the embrace of the inscrutable darkness.[14] That darkness, which is frightening in its authority, appears here in the hardness of heart. That motif pervades this strange text. At every turn, it is affirmed not that Pharaoh's heart is hard, but that Yahweh hardens it. It is Yahweh's peculiar way of bringing the empire to an end. It is Yahweh's odd way to present the possibility of historical freedom. There is more here than can be understood, but whatever else it means it begins in the conviction that God works on both sides of the street. The despairing ones do not see how a newness can come, how evil can be overcome, or how futures can arise from the totalitarian present. This awesome programmatic statement affirms that something is "on the move" in the darkness that even the lord of the darkness does not discern. It is strange that neither Egypt nor Israel understands the movement in the darkness! Israel is no more privy to God's freedom than Egypt is. And when Israel yearns to know too much about that freedom, Israel easily plays the role of Egypt. In any case, this narrative knows that the darkness may be trusted to him as it surely cannot be trusted to Pharaoh. That is energizing because the alternative community dares to affirm how it will turn out. It knows what Pharaoh does not know. It knows, but it does not understand. It knows because it has submitted, and that submission began when the cry was cried toward the free one. There is new energy in finding one who can be trusted with the darkness and who can be trusted to be more powerful than the one who ostensibly rules the light.

Second, in Exod 11:7 there is a wondrous statement of a new reality that surely must energize: "But against any of the people of Israel, either man or beast, not a dog shall growl; that you may know that the Lord makes a distinction between the Egyptians and Israel." In our scholarly ways we may miss the power here. It is too terrible to be contained in a "doctrine of election." It occurs not in a doctrine but in a narrative and an unproven memory that we must let stand in all its audacity. It is not reflective theology but news just for this moment and just for this community. The God who will decide is not the comfortable god of the empire, so fat and well fed as to be neutral and inattentive. Rather, it is the God who is alert to the realities, who does not flinch from taking sides, who sits in the divine council on the edge of his seat and is attentive to his special interests. It is the way of the unifying gods of the empire not to take sides and, by being tolerant, to cast eternal votes for the way things are.

We may pause here to note the kind of theological reflection in which this primal prophetic narrative engages. There is not much here for the reasoned voices. No prophet ever sees things under the aspect of eternity. It is always partisan theology, always for the moment, always for the concrete community, satisfied to see only a piece of it all and to speak out of that at the risk of contradicting the rest of it.[15] Empires prefer reasoned voices who see it all, who understand both sides, and who regard polemics as unworthy of God and divisive of the public good. But what an energizing statement! In his passion and energy, Moses takes sides with losers and powerless marginal people; he has not yet grown cynical with the "double speak" of imperial talk and so dares to speak before the data are in and dares to affront more subtle thinking. The affirmation whispered in the barracks is that Moses is "up front" about his commitments, and Pharaoh is not going to like it.

Seen at a distance, this bald statement is high theology. It is the gospel; *God is for us.* In an empire no god is for anyone. They are old gods who don't care anymore and have tried everything once and have a committee studying all the other issues. For Moses and Israel, energizing comes not out of sociological strategy or hunches about social dynamic, but out of the freedom of God. And so the urging I make to those who would be prophets is that we not neglect to do our work about who God is and that we know our discernment of God is at the breaking points in human community.

Third, the great Song of the Sea (Exod 15:1-18) and Song of Miriam (Exod 15:21) are the most eloquent, liberating, and liberated songs in Israel. The last energizing reality is a doxology in which the singers focus on this free one and in the act of the song appropriate the freedom of God as their own freedom. In his recent typology, David Noel Freedman places this song at the head of the period of militant Mosaic Yahwism.[16] By a study of divine names, he observes the repeated use of the name, the very name of freedom Egypt couldn't tolerate and slaves couldn't anticipate. The speaking of the name already provides a place in which an alternative community can live. So prophets might reflect on the name of God, on what his name is, on what it means, on where it can be spoken, and by whom it might be spoken. There is something direct and primitive about the name in these most primal songs of faith and freedom. Egypt is inclined to hedge the name with adjectives and all manner of qualifiers, but the community of justice practicing the freedom of God cannot wait for all that.

It is of course the case that Moses dominates the tradition and surely has crowded Miriam out of the picture. It is likely that the Song of Moses in Exod 15:1 quotes the Song of Miriam, so that she has priority in the tradition. In the final form of the text it may be that masculine power has crowded out her earlier prominence. In recent time there has been an important scholarly effort to recover Miriam's prominence, suggesting that originally she was an important figure in emerging Israel.[17]

Prophecy cannot be separated very long from doxology, or it will either wither or become ideology. Abraham Heschel has seen most wondrously how doxology is the last full act of human freedom and justice.[18] The prophetic community might ponder what the preconditions of doxology are and what happens when doxologies that address this one are replaced by television jingles that find us singing consumerism ideology to ourselves and to each other. In that world there may be no prophet and surely no freedom. In that world where jingles replace doxology, God is not free and the people know no justice or compassion.

The energy of Moses' doxology includes:

* The speaking of a new name that redefines all social perception.
* A review of an unlikely history of inversion in which imperial reality is nullified. (Obviously that is not the kind of history taught in the royal court school.)

* An asking for the enactment of freedom in dance, freedom in free bodies that Pharaoh could no longer dominate (15:20). (We may ponder the loss of freedom for our bodies and about the ideological dimensions of the current wrath about human sexuality.)

* A culmination in enthronement, the assertion of the one reality Egypt could not permit or tolerate: "The Lord will reign for ever and ever" (15:18). (We must learn that such doxologies are always polemical; the unstated counter-theme, only whispered, is always "and not Pharaoh.")

It is only a poem, and we might say rightly that singing a song does not change reality. However, we must not say that with too much conviction. The evocation of an alternative reality consists at least in part in the battle for language and the legitimization of a new rhetoric. The language of the empire is surely the language of managed reality, of production and schedule and market. But that language will never permit or cause freedom because there is no newness in it. Doxology is the ultimate challenge to the language of managed reality, and it alone is the universe of discourse in which energy is possible.[19]

It is worth asking how the language of doxology can be practiced in the empire. Only where there is doxology is there any emergence of compassion, for doxology cuts through the ideology that pretends to be a given. Only where there is doxology can there be justice, for such songs transfigure fear into energy.

I shall not now explore further the second and third Mosaic memories of sojourn and Sinai, although that is worth doing. The wilderness theme asks about immobilizing satiation; the Sinai theme speaks of God's freedom for the neighbor. Taken altogether, the Mosaic tradition affirms three things:

1. The alternative life is lived in this very particular historical and historicizing community.
2. This community criticizes and energizes by its special memories that embrace discontinuity and genuine breaks from imperial reality.
3. This community, gathered around the memories, knows it is defined by and is at the disposal of a God who as yet is unco-opted and uncontained by the empire.

2

Royal Consciousness:
Countering the Counterculture

We have tried to suggest that Moses was mainly concerned with the formation of a countercommunity with a counterconsciousness. In making that claim for Moses I have carefully avoided any primary link between prophetic imagination and social action, for I believe that Moses did not engage in anything like what we identify as social action. He was not engaged in a struggle to transform a regime; rather, his concern was with the consciousness that undergirded and made such a regime possible. I do not deny that specific actions of a political kind are at times mandatory according to the gospel. But they are not inherently linked to nor the focus of prophetic ministry any more than is a hospital call or a service of worship. Moses was also concerned not with societal betterment through the repentance of the regime but rather with totally dismantling it in order to permit a new reality to appear. Prophetic imagination as it may be derived from Moses is concerned with matters political and social, but it is as intensely concerned with matters linguistic (how we say things) and epistemological (how we know what we know)—all of which may be to engage simply in verbal distinctions. But I stress the point for two reasons; first because the prophetic purpose is much more radical than social change; and second because the issues that concern the Mosaic tradition are much more profound than the matters we usually regard as social action.

The alternative consciousness of Moses was exceedingly radical in its implications both for religion and for the social and political order. First, the notion of God's freedom probably is more than any religious movement can sustain for very long. As Karl Barth has seen, the dispute between revelation and reason concerns not only other or false religions but the very "religion of Christian revelation." Second, the notion of human justice and compassion is rarely a foremost factor in ordering a community. Indeed, most communities find ways of treating it as the last question and never the first question about human reality. It could well be that the possibilities emergent from the ministry of Moses are too radical for any historical community, either in terms of theological presupposition or in terms of societal implementation.

By way of analogy, it is clear that the militancy and radicalness of the earliest churches was soon compromised. Indeed, John Gager has argued that if they had not changed to embrace culture to some extent, they would have disappeared as a sectarian oddity.[1] Perhaps it must be concluded that the vision emerging from Moses is viable only in an intentional community whose passion for faith is knowingly linked to survival in the face of a dominant, hostile culture. That is, such a radical vision is most appropriate to a sectarian mood, which is marginal in the community. Such situations of risk do seem to call forth such radicalness. Conversely, situations of cultural acceptance breed accommodating complacency.

Thus, in our utilization of sociological insight concerning the social dimensions of knowledge, language, and power, we must not be inattentive to our very own sociology and the ways in which it commandeers both our faith and our scholarship.[2] Perhaps the minority community of slaves and midwives was able to affirm the freedom of God just because there was no other legitimated way to stand over against static triumphal religion, for every other less-free God had already been co-opted. Perhaps the minority community of slaves is able to affirm the politics of justice and compassion because there is no other social vision in which to stand in protest against the oppression of the situation. As George Mendenhall has urged, the social purpose of a really transcendent God is to have a court of appeal against the highest courts and orders of society around us.[3] Thus a truly free God is essential to marginal people if they are to have a legitimate standing ground against the oppressive orders of the day. But then it follows that for those who regulate and benefit from the order of the day a truly free God is not necessary, desirable, or perhaps even possible.

Given the social setting of most churches in America, these matters may give us serious pause. It seems probable that the radicalness of the Mosaic phenomenon cannot be separated from the social setting of the *hapiru*.[4] From that it may follow that the freedom of God and the politics of justice are not so easily embraced among us, given our social setting and our derivative religious interestedness. We know enough to know that our best religion is never disinterested. Here I mean only to raise the difficult point that Mosaic, prophetic religion also is not disinterested. Indeed, that tradition of ministry can hardly be understood or practiced without embracing the interests it serves.

All of that is by way of introduction to the emergence of a deep problem in the faith and history of Israel. The revolution, both religious and political, of Moses was able to sustain itself until approximately 1000 B.C.E. as a viable social reality. That is no mean feat when we reflect on the difficulties of maintaining recent revolutions in our own history, for example, the American, French, Russian, Chinese, Vietnamese, Cuban, and Nicaraguan. By the time of Solomon in approximately 962 B.C.E. (after forty years of shrewd and ambiguous leadership from David) there was a radical shift in the foundations of Israel's life and faith. While the shift had no doubt begun and been encouraged by David, the evidence is much clearer and unambiguous with Solomon.[5] The entire program of Solomon now appears to have been a self-serving achievement with its sole purpose the self-securing of the king and dynasty. It consists of what Alberto Soggin calls a program of state-sponsored syncretism, which of course means the steady abandonment of the radicalness of the Mosaic vision. It includes:

1. A harem, which, in addition to serving as a way of facilitating political marriages, likely reflects a concern for self-generated fertility (1 Kgs 11:1-3). (The purpose of a harem in terms of self-securing may be understood quite in contrast to the fortunes of the midwives of the Mosaic period [Exod 1:15-22].)

2. A system of tax districts in which the displacement of clans and tribes made state control more effective (1 Kgs 4:7-19). (Indeed, the deliberate eradication of the tribal perception was essential to the statism of Solomon.) This also shifts the economic weight from local, domestic economies to the political economy of the state.

3. An elaborate bureaucracy, which, in imitation of the larger empires, served to institutionalize technical reason (1 Kgs 4:1-6; 9:23). (And of course technical reason is inherently conservative and nearly immune to questions of justice and compassion.)

4. A standing army so that armaments no longer depended on public opinion and authentic national interest (1 Kgs 4:4; 9:22), not to mention the old notion of the rush of God's Spirit.

5. A fascination with wisdom, which, in addition to imitating the great regimes, represented an effort to rationalize reality, that is, to package it in manageable portions (1Kgs 4:29-34; 10:1-5, 23-25; Prov 1:1; 10:1).[6]

6. Conscripted labor from the villages to support massive building projects (palace, temple, royal cities), quarrying, mining, logging, and shipbuilding (1 Kgs 5:13-19; 6:1—7:51; 9:15-19, 26).

All these things in the Solomonic moment transpired under the effective umbrella of the Jerusalem temple, surely the quintessence of Canaanization in Israel.[7] George Mendenhall has rightly characterized the Solomonic achievement as the "paganization of Israel," that is, a return to the religious and political presuppositions of the pre-Mosaic imperial situation—which is to say that the Solomonic effort was not only abandonment of the revolution but a knowing embrace of pre-prophetic reality.[8] (It is worth noting how our perceptions move. The very developments that Mendenhall describes as "paganization" are those that in another context Gerhard von Rad[9] and others, including myself, have termed "Enlightenment." It is worth recalling this in order to see that more than one reading of the data is possible. Indeed, my own reading of it, from the perspective of the prophetic tradition, is very different from what I have done in other circumstances from a quite different perspective.)[10]

The shift in presuppositions brought about by Solomon can hardly be overestimated. It is likely that David, genius that he was, managed to have it both ways, and, as Stefan Heym has observed, there is a greatness in David that Solomon could only imitate and even then to poor effect.[11] In any case, it is clear that Solomon had a social vision contradictory to that of Moses. The possibility of an alternative consciousness or an alternative community was quite removed from Israel in Solomon's time. The king characteristically could find no such notion acceptable. It seems likely that criticism could no longer be practiced because the transcendent agent necessary to criticism was gone. And we may hypothesize that promises that could energize are now all confiscated for royal use. Solomon was able to create a situation in which everything was already given, in which no more futures could be envisioned because everything was already present a hundredfold. The tension between a criticized present and an energizing future is overcome. There is only an uncriticized and unenergizing present. It follows, of course, that the Mosaic vision of reality nearly disappeared.

In this context, I want to explore three dimensions of the Solomonic achievement that are important to our general thesis. These three elements summarize the dominant culture against which the prophets are regularly a counterpoint.

Affluence

The Solomonic achievement was one of incredible well-being and affluence:

> Judah and Israel were as many as the sand by the sea; they ate and drank and were happy. Solomon ruled over all the kingdoms from the Euphrates to the land of the Philistines and to the border of Egypt; they brought tribute and served Solomon all the days of his life.
>
> Solomon's provision for one day was thirty cors of fine flour, and sixty cors of meal, ten fat oxen, and twenty pasture-fed cattle, a hundred sheep, besides harts, gazelles, roebucks, and fatted fowl. (1 Kgs 4:20-23)

Clearly, there is a new reality in Israel. Never before had there been enough consumer goods to remove the anxiety about survival. The counterculture of Moses lived in a world of scarcity, whether one talks about hurriedly eaten unleavened bread (Exod 12:8-11) or the strange gift of manna from heaven in the wilderness (Exodus 16). And all it takes to counter that consciousness, as kings have always known, is satiation. It is difficult to keep a revolution of freedom and justice under way when there is satiation. (In our own economy, questions of civil rights seem remote when we are so overly fed. And when we look at the former Soviet Union, how strange it is that the burning issues of freedom have become agendas for consumer goods.) That is what is going on in Solomonic Israel. The high standard of living claimed by the text is fully supported by the archaeology of the period. The artifacts, walls, and building remains attest to a well-ordered and secure social situation.

It is nonetheless reasonable to conjecture that the affluence and prosperity so attested is not democratically shared. The menu report of 1 Kings 4 just cited most likely represented only the eating habits and opportunities of the royal entourage, which, at best, was indifferent to the plight of the royal subjects. And then or now, eating that well means food is being taken off the table of another. This notice in 1 Kings 4 suggests that satiation had become an accessible goal for the royal society. Covenanting that takes brothers and sisters seriously had been replaced by consuming, which regards brothers and sisters as products to be used. And in a consuming society an alternative consciousness is surely difficult to sustain.

Oppressive Social Policy

The Solomonic achievement was in part made possible by *oppressive social policy*. Indeed, this was the foundation of the regime and surely the source of the affluence just mentioned. That affluence was undoubtedly hierarchical and not democratic in its distribution. Obviously some people lived well off the efforts of others, for we are reminded that there were those "who built houses and did not live in them, who planted vineyards, and did not drink their wine." Fundamental to social policy was the practice of forced labor, in which at least to some extent subjects existed to benefit the state or the political economy. It is not terribly important or helpful to determine if the forced labor policy included all subjects, as suggested in 1 Kgs 5:13-18, or if the people of Israel were exempted from the general levy of the empire, as contended in 1 Kgs 9:22. In any case, it was unmistakably the policy of the regime to mobilize and claim the energies of people for the sake of the court and its extravagant needs.

As we know from our own recent past, such an exploitative appetite can develop insatiable momentum so that, no matter how much in the way of goods or power or security is obtained, it is never enough. The rebellion announced in 1 Kgs 11:28 and the dispute of 1 Kings 12 concerning the nature of government and the role of people and leaders both show the struggle with a new self-understanding. In that new consciousness on which the regime was built but which was also created by the regime, the politics of justice and compassion has completely disappeared. The order of the state was the overriding agenda, and questions of justice and freedom, the main program of Moses, were necessarily and systematically subordinated. Justice and freedom are inherently promissory; but this regime could not tolerate promises, for they question the present oppressive ordering and threaten the very foundations of current self-serving.

Static Religion

The economics of affluence and the politics of oppression are the most characteristic marks of the Solomonic achievement. But these by themselves could not have prospered and endured as they did had they not received theological sanction. So the third foundational element I suggest is *the establishment of a controlled, static religion* in which God and his temple have become part of the royal landscape, in which the sovereignty of God is fully subordinated to the purpose of the king. In Jerusalem in this period there is a radical revision in the character of God. Now God is fully accessible to the king who is his patron, and the freedom of God is completely overcome. It is almost inconceivable that the God domiciled in Jerusalem would ever say anything substantive or abrasive. Two observations need to be made here. First, I agree with those scholars who stress the tension between the Mosaic and royal traditions. I do not believe the one is derived from the other but rather that they have different roots and foster quite different visions of reality. Second, the reasons for the disastrous religious achievement of Solomon, I believe, are sociological and not historical. That is, Solomon had this kind of shrine not because he inherited it from the Canaanites or Jebusites but because he adopted and developed it because it served his social ideology. If it had not been inherited from the older Canaanite shrine as he might have done, he would have easily imported it as he obviously did so many things he needed for his purposes.

In responsible biblical faith the freedom of God is always in considerable tension with the accessibility of God.[12] This tension was sharp for Moses, who tended to stress the freedom of God at the expense of his accessibility. With Solomon that tension has been completely dissolved in the interest of accessibility. Now there is no notion that God is free and that he may act apart from and even against this regime. Now God is totally and unquestionably accessible to the king and those to whom the king grants access. This new dissolution of the tension is asserted in the old poem of reliable presence:

> The LORD has set the sun in the heavens,
>> but has said that he would dwell in thick darkness.
> I have built thee an exalted house,
>> a place for thee to dwell in forever. (1 Kgs 8:12-13)

God is now "on call," and access to him is controlled by the royal court. Such an arrangement clearly serves two interlocking functions. On the one hand, it assures ready sanction to every notion of the king because there can be no transcendent resistance or protest. On the other hand, it gives the king a monopoly so that no marginal person may approach this God except on the king's terms. There will be no disturbing cry against the king here.

The tension between God's freedom and God's accessibility is a tricky issue that every religious person and especially ministers would do well to reflect upon. Indeed, the whole point of having religious functionaries is to assure access. That is the sociological expectation: "Will you say a prayer, pastor?" It is a burdensome irony that the bearer of the same office is the one called to assert the freedom of God that tempers the notion of accessibility. As it concerns Solomon, this tricky issue is resolved in an undialectical fashion. This poem, commonly regarded as in fact from the dedication of the temple, has God now as a permanent resident in Jerusalem. Any abrasion on the part of this God is unthinkable and untenable.

I believe that these three factors necessarily go together and that no one of them would occur or endure without the other two:

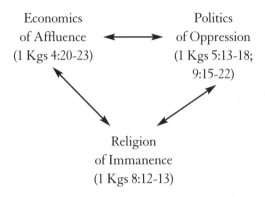

Economics
of Affluence
(1 Kgs 4:20-23)

Politics
of Oppression
(1 Kgs 5:13-18;
9:15-22)

Religion
of Immanence
(1 Kgs 8:12-13)

Obviously, oppressive politics and affluent economics depend on each other. Nevertheless, it is my contention that fundamental to both is the religion of the captive God in which all over-againstness is dissipated and the king and his ideology are completely at ease in the presence of God. When that tension concerning God's freedom has been dissolved, religion easily becomes one more dimension, albeit an important one, for the integration of society. That was not new, and Solomon is hardly to be celebrated for his appreciation of religion. The oppressive pharaohs before him, of course, never doubted the importance of religion, but it was a religion of compatibility in which abrasion was absent. It provided a God who was so present to the regime and to the dominant consciousness that there was no chance of over-againstness; and where there was no over-againstness, there was no chance of newness. This, of course, is discerned as a danger and a threat.

This God is no court of appeal for the marginal ones over against the king, for he is now completely beholden to the king. The essential criticism of Marx is obviously pertinent here. It is precisely religion that legitimates and makes possible the economics and politics that emerged. And prophetic faith knows that if a criticism is to be mounted, it must begin in the unfreedom of God, which in turn results in a royal order quite free now to serve its own narrow interests.

Solomon was able to counter completely the counterculture of Moses.

1. He countered *the economics of equality* with *the economics of affluence*. The contrast is clear and sharp. Mosaic experience had this kind of vision: "He that gathered much had nothing over, and he that gathered little had no lack; each gathered according to what he could eat (Exod 16:18). Here there is no thought of surplus and the accumulation of consumer goods, for that is all over by the time one sits at the royal table in Jerusalem.

2. He countered *the politics of justice* with *the politics of oppression*. Mosaic experience had this kind of vision:

> And if your brother becomes poor, and cannot maintain himself with you, you shall maintain him; as a stranger and a sojourner he shall live with you. Take no interest from him or increase, but fear your God; that your brother may live beside you. . . . For they are my servants, whom I brought forth out of the land of Egypt; they shall not be sold as slaves. (Lev 25:35-42)

That is all over by the time Solomon gets around to forced labor to enhance his rule.

3. He countered *the religion of God's freedom* with *the religion of God's accessibility*. Mosaic experience had this kind of vision of God's freedom. Moses had insisted on God's presence: "Is it not in your going with us, so that we are distinct, I and your people, from all other people that are upon the face of the earth?" (Exod 33:16). But Yahweh answers in his uncompromising freedom, "I will be gracious to whom I will be gracious, and will show mercy on whom I will show mercy. But . . . you cannot see my face; for man shall not see me and live" (Exod 33:19-20).

Solomon managed what one would think is not possible, for he had taken the Mosaic innovation and rendered it null and void. In tenth-century Jerusalem it is as though the whole revolution and social experiment had not happened. The long sequence of imperial history went on as though it had not been interrupted by this revelation of the liberating God. Solomon managed a remarkable continuity with the very Egyptian reality that Moses had sought to counter.

It need hardly be added that the Solomonic regime was able to silence criticism. There are two ways to silence criticism. One is the way of heavy-handed prohibition that is backed by forceful sanction. The treatment of Jeroboam in 1 Kgs 11:40 suggests this way of handling criticism, which is consistent with the style of bloodbath with which the long reign began (1 Kings 2). It is curious that, given the extended criticism of Ahijah the prophet in 1 Kings 11, Solomon makes no response. Indeed, the prophet is ignored. That is the second way of handling criticism: develop a natural immunity and remain totally impervious to criticism. The narrator seems to present that response of cold, resistant silence in deliberate irony. The same response is evident after the strong warning of 1 Kgs 9:1-9. Immediately the narrative responds: "At the end of twenty years in which Solomon had built two houses . . . King Solomon gave to Hiram twenty cities in the land of Galilee" (9:10-11). The royal consciousness was completely contained. Criticism had no viable alternative ground and did not need to be taken seriously. If Solomon had had television at his disposal, he would have managed to buy the harshest critics and make them talk-show celebrities.

There is no concrete evidence about the loss of energy in the regime. Indeed, the narrative suggests a remarkable level of energy toward all kinds of state developments, especially in economics and architecture. But one may at least wonder about the "happiness" of Solomon's community (1 Kgs 4:20; 10:8), which reflects the happiness of satiation. It is at least thinkable that happiness characterized by satiation is not the same as the joy of freedom. It is evident that immunity to any transcendent voice and disregard of neighbor leads finally to the disappearance of passion. And where passion disappears there will not be any serious humanizing energy.[13]

While the late critical dating of Ecclesiastes is not to be doubted, one may hypothesize that the tradition was intuitively correct in assigning that teaching to Solomon.[14] I believe that the mood of world-weariness, satiation, boredom, and vanity in that literature is reflective of the Solomonic situation. To the extent that Ecclesiastes reflects a situation of alienation, it likely speaks of a situation like that of Solomon. Solomon had set out to counter the world of Moses' community of liberation and he had done so effectively. He had traded a vision of freedom for the reality of security. He had banished the neighbor for the sake of reducing everyone to servants. He had replaced covenanting with consuming, and all promises had been reduced to tradable commodities. Every such trade-off made real energy less likely.

That is to make a harsh judgment upon a cultural reality that can, on the other hand, make certain positive claims for itself. But we are not engaged in a study of the royal consciousness on its own terms. We are here considering the meaning of prophetic alternative, an alternative to a social world void of criticism and energy. At the same time, we must at least pay attention to the theological contribution of this period in order to be alert to what is there so as not to overstate the prophetic perspective.

We may discern two major theological contributions from the period, both of which are important for biblical faith and for the Christian tradition. First, there is little doubt that *creation faith* is fully and formally articulated by the Jerusalem establishment.[15] Viewed negatively, creation faith is royal propaganda, daring to claim that the king–temple–royal city complex is the guarantor of both social and cosmic order, and that center of reality protects persons and communities from the dangers of anarchy. Positively, creation faith speaks to a community that has lost interest in survival questions and that is prepared to think more broadly about large issues of proportion, symmetry, and coherence. Thus it is precisely creation faith that rescues the Bible from a parochial discernment of human issues. However, from the point of view of the prophets, we are put on notice. In fact, creation faith tended to give questions of order priority over questions of justice. It tended to value symmetry inordinately and wanted to silence the abrasive concerns of the have-nots. It wanted to overlook the angularities of historical brothers and sisters and focus on large issues over which the king would preside. Hence, a prophetic alternative knows that creation faith brings with it certain costs and that these costs are paid by marginal people who do not figure in the ordering done by the king.

This, of course, is not to imagine that creation faith was first articulated in tenth-century Israel, for there are certainly older evidences. But it does seem likely that in the tenth century creation faith first received its programmatic statement in Israel. As the Mosaic community had sought and worked a sharp discontinuity with the imperial consciousness, now the theological enterprise involved a return to those very imperial perceptions and concerns.

Second, this period obviously features the emergence of *messianism,* that is, the presentation of the Davidic king not only as an important historical accident but also as a necessary agent of God's ultimate purposes. Positively, the Davidic king is understood as an advocate for the marginal ones and so potentially figures as an agent of the Mosaic vision.[16] Negatively and more realistically, as the king takes on increasing significance and power and is assigned an enduring role in the purposes of God, the primary vision becomes the well-being and enhancement of the king per se and not the role of advocate for the marginal. The meaning of kingship could have gone in either direction, but in practice it became not an office of advocacy for the powerless but an agent of greater exploitation by the powerful. Prophetic consciousness thereby is put on notice against every historical agent that assigns to itself enduring, even ontological, significance.

Both *creation faith* and *messianism* have the potential of making major positive contributions to the life and faith of Israel. Both could have advanced the vision and promise of Moses. Creation faith might have articulated a vision of a just cosmic and social order. Messianism could have promised a reliable, powerful advocate for the powerless. In fact, both had intrinsically reactionary tendencies that functioned to enhance the status quo and to resist the abrasive covenantal questions. Thus, not only economically and politically but also theologically, tenth-century monarchic Israel moved against the revolution for the freedom of God and the politics of justice and freedom.

It may be that I have schematized matters too much, but I believe that schematization is evident in the text itself. The emergence of royal reality could have gone either way, and the tradition holds out a hope for faithful royal reality, even as late as Josiah (c. 640–609 B.C.E.). In fact, it did not turn out that way, and that indeed presents a major problem for biblical faith. Royal reality rode roughshod over Moses' vision. The gift of freedom was taken over by the yearning for order. The human agenda of justice was utilized for security. The god of freedom and justice was co-opted for an eternal now. And in place of passion comes satiation.

I believe that the possibility of passion is a primary prophetic agenda and that it is precisely what the royal consciousness means to eradicate. We do not need to review the literature of passion but only to make reference to Soelle, Moltmann, Wiesel, and especially Heschel.[17] Passion as the capacity and readiness to care, to suffer, to die, and to feel is the enemy of imperial reality. Imperial economics is designed to keep people satiated so that they do not notice. Its politics is intended to block out the cries of the denied ones. Its religion is to be an opiate so that no one discerns misery alive in the heart of God. Pharaoh, the passive king in the block universe, in the land without revolution or change or history or promise or hope, is the model king for a world that never changes from generation to generation. That same fixed, closed universe is what every king yearns for—even Solomon in all his splendor.

This model of royal consciousness does not require too much interpretation to be seen as a characterization of our own cultural situation. I have no need to be too immediately "relevant" about these matters, for the careful discernment of these texts will in any case illuminate our own situation. So I offer this paradigm with the prospect that it may indeed help us understand our own situation more effectively. It takes little imagination to see ourselves in this same royal tradition.

 * Ourselves in an economics of affluence in which we are so well off that pain is not noticed and we can eat our way around it.
 * Ourselves in a politics of oppression in which the cries of the marginal are not heard or are dismissed as the noises of kooks and traitors.
 * Ourselves in a religion of immanence and accessibility, in which God is so present to us that his abrasiveness, his absence, his banishment are not noticed, and the problem is reduced to psychology.

Perhaps you are like me, so enmeshed in this reality that another way is nearly unthinkable. The dominant history of that period, like the dominant history of our own time, consists in briefcases and limousines and press conferences and quotas and new weaponry systems. And that is not a place where much *dancing* happens and where no *groaning* is permitted.

We are seldom aware that a minority report may be found in the Bible, the vision of some fanatics who believe that the royal portrayal of history is not accurate because it does not do justice (*sic*) either to this God or to these brothers and sisters.

In the imperial world of Pharaoh and Solomon, the prophetic alternative is a bad joke either to be squelched by force or ignored in satiation. But we are a haunted people because we believe the bad joke is rooted in the character of God himself, a God who is not the reflection of Pharaoh or of Solomon. He is a God with a name of his own, which cannot be uttered by anyone but him. He is not the reflection of any, for he has his own person and retains that all to himself. He is a God uncredentialed in the empire, unknown in the courts, unwelcome in the temple. And his history begins in his attentiveness to the cries to the marginal ones. He, unlike his royal regents, is one whose person is presented as passion and pathos, the power to care, the capacity to weep, the energy to grieve and then to rejoice. The prophets after Moses know that his caring, weeping, grieving, and rejoicing will not be outflanked by royal hardware or royal immunity because this one is indeed God. And kings must face that.

So this is the paradigm I suggest for the prophetic imagination: a royal consciousness committed to achievable satiation.[18] An alternative prophetic consciousness devoted to the pathos and passion of covenanting. The royal consciousness with its program of achievable satiation has redefined our notions of humanness, and it has done that to all of us. It has created a subjective consciousness concerned only with self-satisfaction. It has denied the legitimacy of tradition that requires us to remember, of authority that expects us to answer, and of community that calls us to care. It has so enthroned the present that a promised future, delayed but certain, is unthinkable.

The royal program of achievable satiation:

* Is fed by a management mentality that believes there are no mysteries to honor, only problems to be solved. This, the Solomonic evidence urges, was not a time of great leadership, heroic battles, or bold initiatives. It was a time governed by the cost-accounting of a management mentality.

* Is legitimated by an "official religion of optimism,"[19] which believes God has no business other than to maintain our standard of living, ensuring his own place in his palace.

* Requires the annulment of the neighbor as a life-giver in our history; it imagines that we can live outside history as self-made men and women.

It is mind-boggling to think that, of the Mosaic innovation, only the prophetic word is mobilized against this compelling reality.

3

Prophetic Criticizing
and the Embrace of Pathos

We have considered as a paradigm for prophetic imagination the formation of a consciousness that is a genuine alternative to the royal consciousness. Now a question must be faced (and it is surely a contemporary question): What would such an alternative consciousness be like? Here I take only the modest step of considering some ways in which the prophets of Israel addressed that task, but behind that explicit consideration we necessarily wonder what we might do given our own situation.

We also are children of the royal consciousness. All of us, in one way or another, have deep commitments to it. So the first question is: How can we have enough freedom to imagine and articulate a real historical newness in our situation? That is not to ask, as Israel's prophets ever asked, if this freedom is realistic or politically practical or economically viable. To begin with such questions is to concede everything to the royal consciousness even before we begin. We need to ask not whether it is realistic or practical or viable but whether it is *imaginable*. We need to ask if our consciousness and imagination have been so assaulted and co-opted by the royal consciousness that we have been robbed of the courage or power to think an alternative thought.

When we move from the primal paradigms to the concreteness of the prophets, we may pause to consider what a prophet is and what a prophet does. I suspect that our own self-concept as would-be prophets is most often too serious, realistic, and even grim. But as David Noel Freedman has observed, the characteristic way of a prophet in Israel is that of poetry and lyric. The prophet engages in futuring fantasy. The prophet does not ask if the vision can be implemented, for questions of implementation are of no consequence until the vision can be imagined. The *imagination* must come before the *implementation*. Our culture is competent to implement almost anything and to imagine almost nothing. The same royal consciousness that makes it possible to implement anything and everything is the one that shrinks imagination because imagination is a danger. Thus every totalitarian regime is frightened of the artist.[1] It is the vocation of the prophet to keep alive the ministry of imagination, to keep on conjuring and proposing futures alternative to the single one the king wants to urge as the only thinkable one.

Indeed, poetic imagination is the last way left in which to challenge and conflict the dominant reality. The dominant reality is necessarily in prose, but to create such poetry and lyrical thought requires more than skill in making rhymes. I am concerned not with the formal aspects of poetry but with the substantive issues of alternative prospects that the managed prose around us cannot invent and does not want to permit. Such an activity requires that in the center of our persons and communities we have not fully embraced the consuming apathy espoused by the royal consciousness. It requires that we have not yet finally given up on the promise spoken over us by the God who is free enough to keep his promises.

I am not talking about local pastors spouting poetry that is an assault on the corporate state. What I mean is that the same realities are at work in every family and every marriage and every community. In our achieved satiation we have neither the wits nor the energy nor the courage to think freely about imagined alternative futures. When we think "prophetic" we need not always think grandly about public tasks. The prophetic task needs to be done wherever there are men and women who will yield to the managed prose future offered them by the king. So, we may ask, if we are to do that alternative constructive task of imagination, if we are to reach more than the most surface group prepared to be "religious," where do we begin? What I propose is this: *The royal consciousness leads people to numbness, especially to numbness about death. It is the task of prophetic ministry and imagination to bring people to engage their experiences of suffering to death.*

In considering the Solomonic achievement, I have been speaking of the fate of the royal consciousness as "numbness" even though I have not used that word. The Solomonic establishment embodies the loss of passion, which is the inability to care or suffer. One has only to compare the grief, anguish, and joy of David (2 Sam 1:19-27; 3:33-34; 12:15-23; 18:33; 19:4; 23:13-17) with the one-dimensional narrative of Solomon to realize something decisive has happened from the father to the son. Here the discussion of numbness concerns apathy, the absence of pathos, whereas in the reflective statement of Ecclesiastes the same experience is expressed as vanity:

> All streams run to the sea,
>> but the sea is not full;
> to the place where the streams flow,
>> then they flow again.
> All things are full of weariness;
>> a man cannot utter it;
> the eye is not satisfied with seeing,
>> nor the ear filled with hearing.
> What has been is what will be,
>> and what has been done is what will be done;
>> and there is nothing new under the sun. (Eccl 1:7-9)[2]

In the language of R. D. Laing, people must simply practice the proper *behavior* because they are no longer able to experience their own *experience*.[3] Clearly, the regime is interested not in what people experience but in their behavior, which can be managed.

More specifically, the royal consciousness is committed to numbness about death. It is unthinkable for the king to imagine or experience the end of his favorite historical arrangements, for they have become fully identified with his own person. Indeed, they are his person, as much as he is or has a person. And therefore his historical arrangements must be invested with a quality of durability if not eternity. Kings need to assign the notion of "forever" to every historical accident over which they preside. Thus it is not thinkable among us that our public institutions should collapse and we must engage in deception and self-deception about our alienations. So we must practice the royal game with our marriages and all serious relations, with our bodies, our age and our health, our nerve, and our commitments.

There is no place in the public domain where failure can be faced. Witness the squirming anguish of Richard Nixon—who was more like us than different from us—during the Watergate investigations, or Bill Clinton in his tortured posturing throughout the impeachment process. Ultimately, we are incapable of facing our own death. All these denials about endings are necessary in the royal community because it is too costly to face and embrace them. It would suggest that we are not in charge, that things will not forever stay the manageable way they are, and that things will not finally all work out. It is the business of kings to attach the word "forever" to everything we treasure. The great dilemma is that religious functionaries are expected to use the same "forever," to attach it to things and make it sound theologically legitimated. But "forever" is always the word of Pharaoh, and as such it is the very word against which Yahweh and Moses did their liberating thing.

In a St. Louis radio station there was a cleaning lady who one day walked through a studio during a program offering advice on marital problems. In an offhand way she simply provided advice on her way to do her work. Her advice turned out to be more sound and clever than what was officially offered, and as a result, she was made a part of the regular programming. Miss Blue became a feature, and the words with which she began and ended were "All is well." Sometimes, depending on the mood of the announcer, she was invited to say it repeatedly, perhaps only to cause a chuckle, probably a bit of mockery, even self-mockery, but also to practice the religion of deception. From the ghetto community out of which she spoke, it could be that "all is well" is a trusting affirmation that enables persons to cope. But when the same phrase is co-opted for the media, it becomes an endorsement of the status quo that serves further to deny and numb. It is like a king who says "forever" to keep all the serious questions in check.

The chant of Miss Blue, now co-opted, is not unlike the mocked statement of Jeremiah concerning the numbed self-deception of the temple: "This is the temple of the LORD, the temple of the LORD, the temple of the LORD" (Jer 7:4). Nor is it unlike Toots Shor, that most famous saloon-keeper who died of cancer. In his last days, when his death was imminent, he said, "I don't want to know what I have." That is a fair summary of the attitude of the royal consciousness—not wanting to know. If we don't know, perhaps it won't happen, and we can pretend a while longer. When I must deny about myself then I can afford to deny about my neighbor as well, and I don't need to know what my neighbor has or doesn't have. I can imagine both my neighbor and myself out of historical existence, and "forever" becomes not an affirmation but a denial.

Bruce Lifton has studied attitudes concerning death in our culture beginning with Hiroshima and Nagasaki and responses to these events.[4] Beyond these he has considered the more general response to living in a world where death is so visible, so daily, so pervasive, and so massive, and yet so unnoticed. Lifton has concluded that we have no adequate way to relate to death's reality and potential, so we deny it with numbness.

Moreover, says Lifton, behind that frightened practice is a symbol gap in which we do not have symbols that are deep or strong enough to match the terror of the reality. What takes place when symbols are inadequate and things may not be brought to public expression is that the experience will not be experienced. Obviously the notion of a symbol gap about the reality of death is pertinent to our theme. The royal consciousness that lacks the symbols for full experience is the same royal consciousness that nullified the symbols in the first place. Those symbols that will release experience and let it be redemptive bring to expression precisely those dimensions of reality that the king fears and cannot subjugate. It is the penchant of kings to nullify all symbols that reveal what is beyond royal administration. And so the power of the king to destroy symbols by reducing them makes necessary the subsequent denial of the experience symbolized.

It must be observed that religious practitioners are often easy and unwitting conspirators with and facilitators of such denial. We become the good-humor men and women, for who among us does not want to rush in and smooth things out, to reassure, to cover the grief?

> Everyone helps his neighbor,
>   And says to his brother, "Take courage!"
> The craftsman encourages the goldsmith,
>   and he who smoothes with the hammer him who strikes the
>   anvil,
> saying of the soldering, "It is good";
>   and they fasten it with nails so that it cannot be moved.
>   (Isa 41:6-7)

In a hospital room we want it to be cheery, and in a broken marriage we want to imagine it will be all right. We bring the lewd promise of immortality everywhere, which is not a promise but only a denial of what history brings and what we are indeed experiencing. In the Christian tradition, having been co-opted by the king, we are tempted to legitimate the denial by offering crossless good news and a future well-being without a present anguish. Such a religion serves the king well, for he imagines he is still king. He imagines that he can manage and that his little sand castle will endure (if you pardon the phrase) "forever."

The task of prophetic imagination is to cut through the numbness, to penetrate the self-deception, so that the God of endings is confessed as Lord. Notice that I suggest for the prophet in a really numbed situation a quite elemental and modest task. That task has three parts:

1. To *offer symbols* that are adequate to confront the horror and massiveness of the experience that evokes numbness and requires denial. The prophet provides a way in which the cover-up and the stonewalling can be ended. This does not mean that symbols are to be invented, for that would be too thin. Rather, it means that the prophet is to reactivate out of our historical past symbols that always have been vehicles for redemptive honesty, for example, "cross over to Shiloh to see what I did," or finally, take another look at Pharaoh.[5] The Exodus symbol, above all, is turned to show for all would-be pharaohs that Exodus is a catastrophic ending of what had seemed forever.

2. To *bring to public expression those very fears and terrors* that have been denied so long and suppressed so deeply that we do not know they are there. The public expression of fear and terror, of course, requires not analytic speech and not the language of coercion but the language of metaphor, so that the expression can be touched at many points by different people. Thus the prophet must speak evocatively to bring to the community the fear and the pain that individual persons want so desperately to share and to own but are not permitted to do so. It is obvious that much caricatured prophetic speech serves only to encourage the suppression rather than to end it. This speech requires neither abrasive rejections nor maudlin assurances but an honest articulation of how it is perceived when seen from the perspective of the passion of God.

3. To *speak metaphorically but concretely about the real deathliness that hovers over us and gnaws within us*, and to speak neither in rage nor with cheap grace, but with the candor born of anguish and passion.[6] The deathliness among us is not the death of a long life well lived but the death introduced in that royal garden of

Genesis 2–3, which is surely a Solomonic story about wanting all knowledge and life delivered to our royal management.[7] That death is manifested in alienation, loss of patrimony, and questing for new satiations that can never satisfy, and we are driven to the ultimate consumerism of consuming each other.

The prophet does not scold or reprimand. The prophet brings to public expression the dread of endings, the collapse of our self-madeness, the barriers and pecking orders that secure us at each other's expense, and the fearful practice of eating off the table of a hungry brother or sister. It is the task of the prophet to invite the king to experience what he must experience, what he most needs to experience and most fears to experience, namely, that the end of the royal fantasy is very near. The end of the royal fantasy will permit a glimpse of the true king who is no fantasy, but we cannot see the real king until the fantasy is shown to be a fragile and perishing deception. Precisely in the year of the death of the so-called king does the prophet and the prophet's company see the real king high and lifted up (Isa 6:1).

I believe that the proper idiom for the prophet in cutting through the royal numbness and denial is *the language of grief,* the rhetoric that engages the community in mourning for a funeral they do not want to admit. It is indeed their own funeral.

I have been increasingly impressed with the capacity of the prophet to use the language of lament and the symbolic creation of a death scene as a way of bringing to reality what the king must see and will not. And I believe that grief and mourning, that crying in pathos, is the ultimate form of criticism, for it announces the sure end of the whole royal arrangement.[8]

Jeremiah

In this context I suggest Jeremiah as the clearest model for prophetic imagination and ministry. He is a paradigm for those who address the numb and denying posture of people who do not want to know what they have or what their neighbors have.

Jeremiah is frequently misunderstood as a doomsday spokes-
man or a pitiful man who had a grudge and sat around crying;
but his public and personal grief was for another reason and
served another purpose. Jeremiah embodies the alternative consciousness of Moses in the face of the denying king.[9] He grieves
the grief of Judah because he knows what the king refuses to
know. It is clear that Jeremiah did not in anger heap scorn on
Judah but rather articulated what was in fact present in the
community whether they acknowledged it or not. He articulated what the community had to deny in order to continue the
self-deception of achievable satiation. He affirmed that all the
satiation was a quick eating of self to death. Jeremiah knew long
before the others that the end was coming and that God had had
enough of indifferent affluence, cynical oppression, and pre-
sumptive religion. He knew that the freedom of God had been
so grossly violated (as in Genesis 2–3) that death was at the door
and would not pass over. The prophets do not ask much or
expect much. In his grieving, Jeremiah asked only that the royal
community face up to its real experience, so close to the end.
What both prophet and king knew was that to experience that
reality was in fact to cease to be king.

The grief of Jeremiah was at two levels. First, it was the grief
he grieved for the end of his people. And that was genuine grief
because he cared about this people and he knew that God cared
about this people. But the second dimension of his grief, more
intense, was because no one would listen and no one would see
what was so transparent to him. So his grief was kept sharp and
painful because he had to face regularly the royal consciousness,
which insisted "peace, peace" when apparently only he knew
there was no peace. I think I do not exaggerate or overstate here.
My judgment is that nearly every situation of ministry includes
this component of deception and the terrible dread of letting our
rule come to an end, whether it is no more than tyranny in a marriage or supervision of my favorite anger or hatred. We want
nothing that secures us to die!

The ministry of grief for Jeremiah is not one of self-pity. Seeing what he saw among his people, it was the only appropriate response. Jeremiah had seen what was there for all to see if only they would look, but the others refused to look, simply denied, and were unable to see. The royal folk had for so long lived in a protective, fake world that their perceptual field was skewed and with their best looking they could not see what was there to see. Isaiah's anticipation had been granted:

> Make the heart of this people fat,
>   and their ears heavy,
>   and shut their eyes;
> lest they see with their eyes,
>   and hear with their ears,
> and understand with their hearts,
>   and turn and be healed. (Isa 6:10)

He need not have worried. To turn and be healed they will not. So in his anguish over what is happening, and in his greater anguish over the wholesale denial, Jeremiah presents his poetry.

My impression is that one could open Jeremiah's poetry almost anywhere and find this ministry of articulated grief. As we explore his words it is important to remember that he lived very near the debacle: the Babylonian exile (beginning in 598 B.C.E.) and the fall of Jerusalem (587 B.C.E.). His passion is, as Abraham Heschel has seen, the passion of this God who knows what time it is (Jer 8:7).[10] God knows, and his prophet knows with him, that it is end time. The king does not know, never knows, what time it is because the king wants to banish time and live in an uninterrupted eternal now. God has time for his people and God insists his people take his time seriously.[11] The church in word and by steeple clock announces what time it is and that we must live in God's time. But the king would have it be like a casino in Las Vegas where there is no clock and no time, no beginning and no end, no time to speak or to answer, but only an enduring and unchanging now.

Consider these ways in which Jeremiah penetrates the numbness of the royal consciousness by articulating the grief it so much wants to deny. The grief is over the death of Judah, the very Judah the kings presumed must live forever:

> My anguish, my anguish! I writhe in pain!
>> Oh, the walls of my heart!
> My heart is beating wildly;
>> I cannot keep silent;
> for I hear the sound of the trumpet,
>> the alarm of war.
> Disaster follows hard on disaster,
>> the whole land is laid waste.
> Suddenly my tents are destroyed,
>> my curtains in a moment. (Jer 4:19-20)

His grief is expressed as a public, visible event—the actual invasion and slaughter of his people. He describes with remarkable vividness a near play-by-play of the disaster as it reaches his own bedroom. Nevertheless, that public event is matched by an internal wrenching in which his heart quakes and storms in fear and his very bowels are gripped by terror.

In the poetry that follows he casts a cosmic image of the end of creation:

> I looked on the earth, and lo, it was waste and void;
>> and to the heavens, and they had no light.
> I looked on the mountains, and lo, they were quaking,
>> and all the hills moved to and fro.
> I looked, and lo, there was no man,
>> and all the birds of the air had fled.
> I looked, and lo, the fruitful land was a desert,
>> and all its cities were laid in ruins,
> before the Lord, before his fierce anger. (Jer 4:23-26)

But the poetry is more than the end of creation. Recall that I have suggested creation is a work guaranteed by the king. The king is the one charged to order and preserve creation, and thus the return to chaos implicitly announces the failure of kingship and its end. There is no creation because there is no king. The very thing that justified kingship has been lost. So whatever else, the royal folk are confronted with a future in which they do not figure.

In the poetry of chapters 8–10, Jeremiah provides a rich supply of metaphors designed to break the numbness. First there is an image about the utter misreading of the situation. There is a time to mourn and a time to dance, a time to weep and a time to laugh (Eccl 3:4); but Judah does not know what time it is:

> Even the stork in the heavens
>   knows her times;
> and the turtledove, swallow, and crane
>   keep the time of their coming;
> but my people know not
>   the ordinance of the Lord. (Jer 8:7; see 4:22)

It is crying time. It is death time and they imagine such time never comes. After a war scenario of charging horses, the prophet turns wistful:

> Is there no balm in Gilead?
>   Is there no physician there?
> Why then has the health of the daughter of my people
>   not been restored?
> O that my head were waters,
>   and my eyes a fountain of tears,
> that I might weep day and night
>   for the slain daughter of my people!
> O that I had in the desert
>   a wayfarer's lodging place,
> that I might leave my people
>   and go away from them! (Jer 8:22—9:2)

In his opening concerning the balm, the prophet asks a question. He does not make an affirmation as in the African American spiritual ("There Is a Balm in Gilead"), but leaves the question unanswered. The second question is asked in deeper pathos: Is there no doctor?[12] Failing an answer he must now deepen his expression of pain. The answer was not given because answering is the way of royal Israel. Now it is time not for answers but for questions that defy answers because the royal answering service no longer functions. Answers from that source presume control and symmetry. And that is gone.

So the prophet speaks his grief at the lack of resolution. He cannot cry enough. More tears need to be cried than his eyes will permit. There is not enough time, even day and night, for this death of all death, "the slain daughter of my people." First there is no answer. Then inadequate tears. And third the wish for flight: "O that I had a place in the desert . . . because they are treacherous, they proceed from evil to evil, that do not know me, says the Lord." The cry, the grief, the pain of death is that of Yahweh. They do not know Yahweh. They do not know how to reckon with the really free one who will cause endings. He fits none of their categories, and they can't "get a handle" on him. So they persist in treating him like every other one; but it brings no relief because he will be God of the endings. He is not to be avoided.

Jeremiah can feel empathy for the royal folk. He yearns for the peace as much as they do. He too wants business as usual, but death has now changed all that: "We looked for peace, but no good came, for a time of healing, but behold, terror" (8:15). This most eloquent of all prophets cannot find words to bring the grief to public expression: "My grief is beyond healing, my heart is sick within me" (8:18). Capacity for clear thinking and faithful deciding has been lost. This is not just a little play-acting for public edification. His whole life has now been claimed to embody the grief of dead Judah. It is the grief Yahweh knows that he would share with his people, but they cannot, and so Jeremiah must answer for his whole people.

In his long and eloquent statement on kings in chapter 22, the prophet has chastened and castigated, commended, and cajoled. After all that, he comes to the tragic boy-king, Jehoiachin, here called Coniah. The boy is innocent but must pay for the dynasty and must bear in his body the punishment of the whole family. He is Judah, exiled Judah, and Jeremiah assigns to him the grief of all Judah.

In 22:28 Jeremiah begins grieving for this one who is innocent and forgotten, with no more claims to make: "Is this man Coniah a despised broken pot, a vessel no one cares for?" Then he issues the most poignant lament in the whole Bible. The whole land is mobilized to grieve the tragedy: "O land, land, land!" (22:29). And then the dynasty is ended: "Write this man down as childless, a man who shall not succeed in his days; for none of his offspring shall succeed . . ." (22:30). The tear in the heart of Jeremiah is unspeakable. He does not gloat or rejoice. He would rather this king could rescue royal Judah—but it is very late.

The prophet knows he is inadequate for the grieving of Israel's death, so he asks for public grief: "Take up weeping and wailing for the mountains, and a lamentation for the pastures of the wilderness" (9:10). In this he echoes the expectation of Amos that what is to happen must be brought to public expression:

> In all the squares there shall be wailing;
>   and in all the streets they shall say, "Alas! alas!"
> They shall call the farmers to mourning
>   and to wailing those who are skilled in lamentation.
>   (Amos 5:16)

Not only did Amos call for grief, but he did so as he presented forsaken ravaged Israel:

> Fallen, no more to rise,
>   is the virgin Israel;

> forsaken on her land,
> > with none to raise her up. (Amos 5:1-2)

That image of a dying one is picked up by Jeremiah and characteristically made more radical, for now the lady is no longer a virgin but a tramp, a whore all dressed up with no place to go:

> And you, O desolate one,
> what do you mean that you dress in scarlet,
> > that you deck yourself with ornaments of gold,
> > that you enlarge your eyes with paint?
> In vain you beautify yourself.
> > Your lovers despise you . . .
> For I heard a cry as of a woman in travail,
> > anguish as of one bringing forth her first child,
> the cry of the daughter of Zion gasping for breath,
> > stretching out her hands,
> Woe is me! I am fainting before murderers. (Jer 4:30-31)

It is like a woman in labor, but there is no birth here, only death; there is the desperate gasping and then there is silence. Judah has ended.

First the prophet states his own grieving. Then he "goes public" and includes the professionals. And then in a remarkable statement he depicts the mother of Israel, beloved Rachel, grieving:[13]

> A voice is heard in Ramah,
> > lamentation and bitter weeping.
> Rachel is weeping for her children;
> > she refuses to be comforted for her children,
> because they are not. (Jer 31:15)

Neither Jeremiah nor his contemporaries are adequate to this grief. It must be done by the one who in anguish gave birth and in anguish now faces her children's death. There is no comfort anymore; not comforted: they are not! The death of the unthinkable end is matched to the birth of the unthinkable miracle of beginning. Now it has been said. They are not; not exile; not punished. Just *not!* And that is beyond either consolation or explanation. This poetry is among the boldest in ancient Israel, for the situation requires audacity. Imagine bringing back mother Rachel to grieve her darling. There can only be grief, for

> Your hurt is incurable,
>   and your wound is grievous.
> There is none to uphold your cause,
>   no medicine for your wound,
>   no healing for you. (Jer 30:12-13)

There can be only death. And then the imagery is pressed to its extremity:

> Is Ephraim my dear son?
>   Is he my darling child?
> For as often as I speak against him,
>   I do remember him still. (Jer 31:20)

Yahweh is grieving and will not turn loose. The language permits the words of Jeremiah to transcend the person of the prophet. This grief will not be dismissed as the idiosyncrasy of Jeremiah, for it is nothing less than God's grief over his dead child.[14] And God would not grieve that death if there were a way to prevent it. There is no assurance or announcement of hope; there is only yearning that is admittedly hope-filled, but it stops short of knowing too much or claiming too much. Jeremiah has pressed where his contemporaries would not readily go, to the pain of God, to a place where only Hosea had ventured before. Yahweh is no longer an enemy who must punish or destroy but the helpless parent who must stand alongside death, like Mary at Calvary, like David over Absalom, "My child, my child," but he is helpless and can only grieve.[15] The drift toward death is so far advanced that none—not king, not temple, not even Yahweh—can keep it from happening. Eventually mercy may be granted, but not before death. At most there is here an enigmatic yearning, even by Yahweh, that history would not take its ruthless course.

The poetry here uses the language of grief as it is characteristically expressed in the poetry of lamentation. There is a sense of forsakenness with none to comfort, with a yearning for mercy, but only a yearning. Israel must be grieved and not too soon can there be a word beyond grief.

Jeremiah spoke to the people with glazed eyes that looked and did not see. They were so encased in their own world of fantasy that they were stupid and undiscerning. And so the numbness was not broken and they continued in their fantasy world: "They have healed the wound of my people lightly, saying, 'Peace, peace,' when there is no peace" (Jer 6:14; 8:11). They fancied their covenantal stupidity to be royal wisdom (8:8) and they went their royal, self-deceiving ways. The prophets imagined that the yoke was a temporary one but not finally serious or decisive (chaps. 27–28). The kings imagined that to void a word and burn a scroll would make the sovereignty of Yahweh "inoperative" (36:23-24). The kings would do everything but grieve, for that is the ultimate criticism and the decisive announcement of dismantling.

We need not press the language of Jeremiah to expect it to be too concrete and specific. The prophet is engaged in a battle for language, in an effort to create a different epistemology out of which another community might emerge. The prophet is not addressing behavioral problems. He is not even pressing for repentance. He has only the hope that the *ache* of God could penetrate the *numbness* of history. He engages not in scare or threat but only in a yearning that grows with and out of pain.

So what is this prophet up to? Why all this grief? Surely he is not like the "tearjerker" minister who believes that a good cry makes a fine funeral. Nor shall we be professional funeral attenders to whom tears come automatically with one verse of "Rock of Ages." But we do know from our own pain and hurt and loneliness that tears break barriers like no harshness or anger. Tears are a way of solidarity in pain when no other form of solidarity remains. And when one addresses numbness clearly, anger, abrasiveness, and indignation as forms of address will drive the hurt deeper, add to the numbness, and force people to behaviors not rooted in experience.

This denying and deceiving kind of numbness is broken only by the embrace of negativity,[16] by the public articulation that we are fearful and ashamed of the future we have chosen. The pain and regret denied only immobilizes. In the time of Jeremiah the pain and regret denied prevented any new movement either from God or toward God in Judah. The covenant was frozen and there was no possibility of newness until the numbness was broken. Jeremiah understood that the criticism must be faced and embraced, for then comes liberation from incurable disease, from broken covenant, and from failed energy. This tradition of biblical faith knows that anguish is the door to historical existence, that embrace of ending permits beginnings. Naturally kings think the door of anguish must not be opened, for it dismantles fraudulent kings. Kings know intuitively that the deception, the phony claims of prosperity, oppression, and state religion will collapse when the air of covenant hits them. The riddle and insight of biblical faith is the awareness that only anguish leads to life, only grieving leads to joy, and only embraced endings permit new beginnings.

Jeremiah stands midway in the history of Israel's grief. Before him, Amos condemned those in their self-deception who were unable and unwilling to grieve (Amos 6:6). After Jeremiah comes Jesus of Nazareth, who understands grief as the ultimate criticism that had to be addressed against Jerusalem (Matt 23:27; Luke 19:41). Jeremiah stands midway and speaks the grief of God that Israel finally must share. Without it there is no newness.

Jesus had understands Jeremiah. Ecclesiastes said only that there is a time to weep and a time to laugh; but Jesus sees that only those who mourn will be comforted (Matt 5:4). Only those who embrace the reality of death will receive the new life. Implicit in his statement is that those who do not mourn will not be comforted and those who do not face the endings will not receive the beginnings. The alternative community knows it need not engage in deception. It can stand in solidarity with the dying, for those are the ones who hope. Jeremiah, faithful to Moses, understood what numb people will never know, that only grievers can experience their experiences and move on.

I used to think it curious that, when having to quote scripture on demand, someone would inevitably say, "Jesus wept." It is usually done as a gimmick to avoid having to quote a longer passage. But now I understand the depth of that verse. Jesus knew what we numb ones must always learn again: (a) that weeping must be real because endings are real; and (b) that weeping permits newness. His weeping permits the kingdom to come. Such weeping is a radical criticism, a fearful dismantling because it means the end of all machismo; weeping is something kings rarely do without losing their thrones. Yet the loss of thrones is precisely what is called for in radical criticism.

4

Prophetic Energizing and the Emergence of Amazement

The ministry of Jeremiah as we have considered it as a model was concerned with radical criticism. And the most radical criticism of the prophet is in *grief over death*. The alternative community embodied in Jeremiah saw how surely fatal everything that the kings called life was. There are, to be sure, other important aspects of Jeremiah's ministry. For example, Thomas Raitt has recently argued persuasively that Jeremiah is the boldest and most inventive of all the prophets of hope.[1] In such a view, different critical questions do arise; but Raitt, after the manner of John Bright,[2] ascribes to Jeremiah substantial parts of the hope poetry. I call attention to this in order not to misrepresent the richness of the Jeremiah tradition.

In any case, my governing hypothesis is that the alternative prophetic community is concerned both with criticizing and energizing. On the one hand, it is to show that the dominant consciousness (which I have termed "royal") will indeed end and that it has no final claim upon us. On the other hand, it is the task of the alternative prophetic community to present an alternative consciousness that can energize the community to fresh forms of faithfulness and vitality. Having considered the first of these tasks in the tradition of Jeremiah, I now turn to the second function of prophecy, to energize. I propose this hypothesis: *The royal consciousness leads people to despair about the power to move toward new life. It is the task of prophetic imagination and ministry to bring people to engage the promise of newness that is at work in our history with God.*

Numb people do not discern or fear death. Conversely, despairing people do not anticipate or receive newness.

Excluding Hope

As a beginning point it may be affirmed that the royal consciousness militates against hope. For those who are denied entry into prosperity a kind of hopelessness emerges because little or no prospect for change is on the horizon. Israel had no doubt that since the Solomonic achievement the royal prosperity was increasingly closed to large numbers of the Israelites. That indeed is a key point in the polemics of Amos. And so, in that time as in our own, the royal arrangement surely and properly evokes despair among those who are shut out.

It is equally important to perceive that those who have entry to power and prosperity are also victims of hopelessness, or in a more contemporary idiom, have a sense of powerlessness. The royal consciousness means to overcome history and therefore by design the future loses its vitality and authority. The present ordering, and by derivation the present regime, claims to be the full and final ordering. That claim means there can be no future that either calls the present into question or promises a way out of it. Thus the fulsome claim of the present arrangement is premised on hopelessness. This insidious form of realized eschatology requires persons to live without hope. The present is unending in its projection, uncompromising in its claim of loyalty, and unaccommodating in having its own way. In the words of a recent beer commercial, you can be totalitarian when "you believe in what you're doing" and you conclude that one way is the "right way." I believe the Solomonic regime created such a situation of despair. Inevitably it had to hold on desperately and despairingly to the present, for if the present slipped away, there would be nothing. The future had already been annulled. I do not find it farfetched to imagine the lack of promise in Ecclesiastes to be pertinent to the royal consciousness:

> What has been is what will be,
>> and what has been done is what will be done;
>> and there is nothing new under the sun.
> Is there a thing of which it is said,
>> "See, this is new"?
> It has been already,
>> in the ages before us. (Eccl 1:9-10)

There is nothing new, partly because nothing seemed to be happening but also because the regime had ordered and decreed it that way. The need to annul the future must lead to a situation in which hope is also denied. In concrete terms, technological, agricultural, and other social advances are impeded in aristocratic monarchies because the taxes, tithes, tribute, tolls, rents, and confiscations drain all the peasants' resources and rationale for creativity; only the technology of warfare advances at a more rapid pace because that contributes to the expansion and control of the king and his entourage.[3] Furthermore, the authority of the king rests on dynastic tradition; so introducing new visions opens the possibility of challenges to the tradition and therefore the king's authority.

No New Beginnings

More specifically, the termination of the present in the fall of 587 B.C.E., just as Jeremiah had anticipated, created a situation in which the royal consciousness found itself without resource. The very kings who could not cope with the thought that an end might come could also not imagine a new beginning. Those who had worked so hard to deny the future and banish hope could not all of a sudden permit hope to happen. It is unthinkable for the king to imagine or experience a really new beginning that is underived or unextrapolated from what went before. Kings were accustomed to new arrangements and new configurations of the same pieces, but the yearning to manage and control means that new intrusions are not regarded as desirable. Neither are they regarded as possible or discerned when they happen. And thus the same royal consciousness that could not imagine endings and so settled for numb denial is the one that could not imagine beginnings and so settled for hopeless despair and a grim endurance of the way things now are. Beginnings are no more thinkable or acceptable to kings than endings are, for both announce an inscrutable sovereignty that kings cannot entertain.

The despair is perhaps reflected in Psalm 137. So I contend that the despair of the early exile is not a new thing in the Babylonian exile; rather, it is the payoff for the hopeless, futureless existence of Israel for a long period. To be sure, the imprecations of Ps 137:7-9 may indicate some quite modest hopefulness; but obviously the poet envisions no bold hope for restoration. At best it is a grim holding, a resolve to remember forever, and a venting of hostility. No word of a beginning that would transform history is articulated here. In the poetry of Lamentations, as Norman Gottwald has observed, hints of hope do poke through;[4] but we should not miss the extreme reservation of the conclusion of the last poem:

> Restore us to yourself, O Lᴏʀᴅ, that we may be restored!
>> Renew our days as of old!
> Or have you utterly rejected us?
>> Are you exceedingly angry with us? (Lam 5:20-21)

There is the risk of a petition, but with little conviction. The last pair of rhetorical questions seems to expect the worst.

The inability to imagine or even tolerate a new intrusion is predictable given the characteristic royal capacity to manage all the pieces. It is so even in our personal lives, in which we conclude that the given dimensions we have frequently rearranged are the only dimensions that exist. To imagine a new gift given from the outside violates our reason. We are able to believe no more in the graciousness of God than we are in the judgment of God.

We are largely confined to reflections on the given pieces, and our modest expectations are confined by our reason, our language, and our epistemology. We have no public arenas in which serious hopefulness can be brought to articulation. What is most needed is what is most unacceptable—an articulation that redefines the situation and that makes way for new gifts about to be given. Without a public arena for the articulation of gifts that fall outside our conventional rationality, we are fated to despair. We know full well the makings of genuine newness are not included among these present pieces. And short of genuine newness life becomes a dissatisfied coping, a grudging trust, and a managing that dares never ask too much.

My judgment is that such a state of affairs not only is evident in the exile of Judah but is characteristic of most situations of ministry. When we try to face the holding action that defines the sickness, the aging, the marriages, and the jobs of very many people, we find that we have been nurtured away from hope, for it is too scary. Such hope is an enemy of the very royal consciousness with which most of us have secured a working arrangement. The question facing ministry is whether there is anything that can be said, done, or acted in the face of the ideology of hopelessness.

Penetrating Despair

The task of prophetic imagination and ministry, especially as we see it in sixth-century Judah, is to cut through the despair and to penetrate the dissatisfied coping that seems to have no end or resolution. A prophet can do little in such a situation of hopelessness, so I suggest a quite basic and modest task. It includes three actions:

Symbols

The offering of symbols that are adequate to contradict a situation of hopelessness in which newness is unthinkable. The prophet has only the means of word, spoken word and acted word, to contradict the presumed reality of his or her community. The prophet is to provide the wherewithal whereby hope becomes possible again to a community of kings who now despair of their royalty. After a time, kings become illiterate in the language of hope. Hope requires a very careful symbolization. It must not be expressed too fully in the present tense because hope one can touch and handle is not likely to retain its promissory call to a new future. Hope expressed only in the present tense will no doubt be co-opted by the managers of this age.

What a commission it is to express a future that none think imaginable! Of course this cannot be done by inventing new symbols, for that is wishful thing. Rather, it means to move back into the deepest memories of this community and activate those very symbols that have always been the basis for contradicting the regnant consciousness. Therefore the symbols of hope cannot be general and universal but must be those that have been known concretely in this particular history.[5] And when the prophet returns, with the community, to those deep symbols, they will discern that hope is not a late, tacked-on hypothesis to serve a crisis but rather the primal dimension of every memory of this community. The memory of this community begins in God's promissory address to the darkness of chaos, to barren Sarah, and to oppressed Egyptian slaves. The speech of God is first about an alternative future.

In offering symbols the prophet has two tasks. One is to mine the memory of this people and educate them to use the tools of hope. The other is to recognize how singularly words, speech, language, and phrase shape consciousness and define reality. The prophet is the one who, by use of these tools of hope, contradicts the presumed world of the kings, showing both that that presumed world does not square with the facts and that we have been taught a lie and have believed it because the people with the hardware and the printing press told us it was that way. And so the offering of symbols is a job not for a timid clerk who simply shares the inventory but for people who know something different and are prepared, out of their own anguish and amazement, to know that the closed world of managed reality is false. The prophetic imagination knows that the real world is the one that has its beginning and dynamic in the promising speech of God and that this is true even in a world where kings have tried to banish all speech but their own.

Hope and Yearning

The task of prophetic imagination and ministry is *to bring to public expression those very hopes and yearnings* that have been denied so long and suppressed so deeply that we no longer know they are there.[6] Hope, on the one hand, is an absurdity too embarrassing to speak about, for it flies in the face of all those claims we have been told are facts. Hope is the refusal to accept the reading of reality which is the majority opinion; and one does that only at great political and existential risk. On the other hand, hope is subversive, for it limits the grandiose pretension of the present,[7] daring to announce that the present to which we have all made commitments is now called into question. Thus the exilic community lacked the tools of hope. The language of hope and the ethos of amazement have been partly forfeited because they are an embarrassment. The language of hope and the ethos of amazement have been partly squelched because they are a threat.

It is mind-boggling to think of the public expression of hope as a way of subverting the dominant royal embrace of despair. I am not talking about optimism or development or evolutionary advances but rather about promises made by one who stands distant from us and over against us but remarkably *for us*. Speech about hope cannot be explanatory and scientifically argumentative; rather, it must be lyrical in the sense that it touches the hopeless person at many different points. More than that, however, speech about hope must be primally theological, which is to say that it must be in the language of covenant between a personal God and a community. Promise belongs to the world of trusting speech and faithful listening. It will not be reduced to the "cool" language of philosophy or the private discourse of psychology. It will finally be about God and us, about his faithfulness that vetoes our faithlessness. Those who would be prophetic will need to embrace that absurd practice and that subversive activity.

The urging to bring hope to public expression is based on a conviction about believing folks. It is premised on the capacity to evoke and bring to expression the hope that is within us (see 1 Pet 3:15). It is there within and among us, for we are ordained of God to be people of hope. It is there by virtue of our being in the image of the promissory God. It is sealed there in the sacrament of baptism. It is dramatized in the Eucharist—"until he come." It is the structure of every creed that ends by trusting in God's promises. Hope is the decision to which God invites Israel, a decision against despair, against permanent consignment to chaos (Isa 45:18), oppression, barrenness, and exile.

Hope is the primary prophetic idiom not because of the general dynamic of history or because of the signs of the times but because the prophet speaks to a people who, willy-nilly, are God's people. Hope is what this community must do because it is God's community invited to be in God's pilgrimage. And as Israel is invited to grieve God's grief over the ending, so Israel is now invited to hope in God's promises. That very act of hope is the confession that we are not children of the royal consciousness.

Of course prophetic hope easily lends itself to distortion. It can be made so grandiose that it does not touch reality; it can be trivialized so that it does not impact reality; it can be "bread and circuses" so that it only supports and abets the general despair. But a prophet has another purpose in bringing hope to public expression, and that is to return the community to its single referent, the sovereign faithfulness of God. It is only that return that enables a rejection of the closed world of royal definition. Only a move from a managed world to a world of spoken and heard faithfulness permits hope. It is that overriding focus that places Israel in a new situation and that reshapes exile, not as an eternal fate but as the place where hope can most amazingly appear. No objective norm can prevent a prophet of hope from being too grandiose or too trivial or simply a speaker for bread and circuses. It is likely that the only measure of faithfulness is that hope always comes after grief and that the speaker of this public expression must know and be a part of the anguish that permits hope. Hope expressed without knowledge of and participation in grief is likely to be false hope that does not reach despair. Thus, as Thomas Raitt has shown, it is precisely those who know death most painfully who can speak hope most vigorously.

Newness That Redefines

The prophet must speak metaphorically about hope but concretely about the real newness that comes to us and redefines our situation. The prophet must speak not only about the abandonment of Israel by its God but about the specificity of Babylon. Talk about newness in exile comes not from a happy piety or from a hatred of Babylon but from the enduring jealousy of Yahweh for his people. This jealousy, so alien to our perceptual world, includes rejection of his people, which sends them and even Yahweh himself into exile. It is a jealousy that stays with his people, making their anguish his anguish and his future their future. The hope that must be spoken is hope rooted in the assurance that God does not quit even when the evidence warrants his quitting. The hope is rooted in God's ability to utilize even the folly of Israel. The memory of this community-about-to-hope revolves around such hope-filled events as that of Cain, the murderer of a brother, being marked protectively; of the chaos of royal disarray resolved in praise; of rejected Joseph observing to his brother that in all things God works for good; of Solomon, very Solomon, born in love to this shabby royal couple—and out of that comes a word that contradicts the exile.

The Language of Amazement

The hope-filled language of prophecy, in cutting through the royal despair and hopelessness, is the language of amazement. It is a language that engages the community in new discernments and celebrations just when it had nearly given up and had nothing to celebrate. The language of amazement is against the despair just as the language of grief is against the numbness. I believe that, rightly embraced, no more subversive or prophetic idiom can be uttered than the practice of doxology, which sets us before the reality of God, of God right at the center of a scene from which we presumed he had fled. Indeed, the language of amazement is the ultimate energizer in Israel, and the prophets of God are called to practice that most energizing language.

Second Isaiah serves as the peculiar paradigm for a prophet of hope to kings in despair. This great poet of the exile understood that speech that rearranges the pieces and that echoes the management mentality of its contemporaries is not worth the bother. Second Isaiah presumably lived through and knew about the pathos of Lamentations and the rage of Job.[8] Nevertheless, he goes beyond pathos and rage to speeches of hope and doxology.

Second Isaiah has indispensable precursors in Jeremiah and Ezekiel, as Thomas Raitt has made clear. But more than these or any other, it is Second Isaiah who announces to exiled Judah a genuine innovation. His announcement depends first of all on the audacity of his person and his poetry. He must have been a remarkable person to say things that violated the entire perceptual field of his community. Second, his speaking depends on the reality that his time was indeed a newness of time in which all the old certitudes were becoming unglued. Babylon was going and Persia was coming, and this poet knew precisely what time it was. Third, and most important, his speaking depends on the reality and confession of God's radical freedom, freedom not only from the conceptions and expectations of his people but from God's own past actions as well. God, much like Reinhold Niebuhr, does have courage to change.[9] His freedom is not some pious or spiritual event, for God's freedom is visible in the public place. In speaking of forgiveness Raitt says: "Jeremiah and Ezekiel commenced communicating a revolutionary shift in God's will and plan for his people in history . . . a new 'game' or dispensation has begun. . . . God is operating under a new plan."[10] This is Second Isaiah's first word to the exiles, a word of forgiveness:

> Comfort, comfort my people, says your God.
> Speak tenderly to Jerusalem,
>   and cry to her
> that her warfare is ended,
>   that her iniquity is pardoned. (Isa 40:1-2)

The discomforted are comforted. This is not a word in a vacuum or a general theory about a gracious God. The poet responds precisely and concretely. He responds to Jeremiah's Rachel who refuses to be comforted (Jer 31:15). He speaks directly to and against the poems of Lamentations that found "none to comfort" (Lam 1:2, 16, 17, 21). To find comfort in exile is not thinkable, but in this remarkable beginning the poet refuses all that. The free God is ending that whole situation and now enacts an amnesty that was unthinkable before the speech. That speech let Israel know what she did not know before he spoke. Hope is created by speech, and before that speech Israel was always hopeless. Indeed, are we not all? Before we are addressed, we know no future and no possible newness. Where there is no speech we must live in despair. And exile is first of all where our speech has been silenced and God's speech has been banished. But the prophetic poet asserts hope precisely in exile.

The hope announced is not a nice feeling or a new inner spiritual state. Rather, it is grounded in a radical discernment of Israel's worldly situation. The poet employs a radical *political* announcement twice. First he instructs the watchman to announce a new reality:

> Get you up to the high mountain,
>   O Zion, herald of good tidings;
> lift up your voice with strength,
>   O Jerusalem, herald of good tidings,
>   lift it up, fear not;
> say to the cities of Judah,
>   "Behold your God!"
> Behold, the Lord God comes with might. (Isa 40:9-10)

Note that the prophet may have been afraid to say such an absurd and subversive word, but he is not to fear; he is to make this exile-transforming announcement. The new reality is that the One who seemed to be dismissed as useless and impotent has claimed his throne. And he has done so right in exile; right under the nose of the Babylonians. The poet brings Israel to an enthronement festival, even as Jeremiah had brought Israel to a funeral. Whereas that scenario left Israel in consuming grief, Second Isaiah brought Israel to new buoyancy. Whereas Jeremiah tried to penetrate the *numbness,* Second Isaiah had to deal with *despair.* Both had to speak out of Moses' liberating tradition against the royal mentality that would not let people grieve or hope.

We should hold to the metaphor of enthronement and not leave it too soon or reduce it too concretely. The poet is not changing external politics but is reclaiming Israel's imagination. He asserts a newness that is so old Israel had forgotten, but it is there in memory. Moses' energizing Song of the Sea ended with enthronement: "The LORD will reign for ever and ever" (Exod 15:18). It is as though Second Isaiah means to bring Israel back to the doxology of Moses, but it is not only a memory recalled. It is a seizure of power in this moment that carries with it the delegitimizing of all other claimants and definers of reality. The other claimants to power and definers of reality are, in this act of language, like the ancient Egyptians, dead upon the seashore. This public act of poetic articulation reshapes Israel's destiny. Exile with the crowned sovereign is very different from kingless exile because it means the grimness is resolvable.

And what a god has now claimed his rule! He is as terrifyingly masculine as a warrior with sleeves rolled up for battle and as gently maternal as a carrier of a lamb. It is all there—for exiles. It includes the comfort of enormous power, with stress on *fort* (strengthen); it includes the comfort of nurture, with stress on *com* (along with). Israel is in a new situation where singing is possible again. Have you ever been in a situation where because of anger, depression, preoccupation, or exhaustion you could not sing? And then you could? Change resulted from being addressed, called by a name, cared for, recognized, and assured. The prophet makes it possible to sing and the empire knows that people who can boldly sing, have not accepted the royal definition of reality. If the lack of singing is an index of exile, then we are in it, for we are a people who scarcely can sing. The prophet makes the hopefulness of singing happen again. The second enthronement formula is even more familiar:

> How beautiful upon the mountains
> > are the feet of him who brings good tidings . . .
> > who publishes salvation,
> > who says to Zion, "Your God reigns." (Isa 52:7)

The very one who seems to have lost charge is in charge now. The one who seemed to end in grief and bankruptcy in Jeremiah is the one who now will invert history. And the poet knows well that the inversion to real power happens only by suffering (49:14-15). The rejoicing belongs to those who know about the abandonment and the pathos. It is a curious route to kingship, but that is how it comes in Israel's history.

The effect of Second Isaiah is to energize Israel to fresh faith. But notice the radical, bold, even revolutionary form energizing takes. The prophet employs no psychological gimmicks and no easy meditative steps because the issues are not private, personal, spiritual, or internal. The only serious energizing needed or offered is the discernment of God in all his freedom, the dismantling of the structures of weariness, and the dethronement of the powers of fatigue. (Jesus, in his sayings concerning weariness and rest and changing yokes [Matt 11:28-30] is faithful to Second Isaiah.) Lament is the loss of true kingship, whereas doxology is the faithful embrace of the true king and the rejection of all the phony ones.

As is often suggested, I suggest that these two enthronement formulas of Isa 40:9-11 and 52:7 are the fount from which comes the rest of the poetry. The remainder is an exegesis of this kingship freshly asserted. It is the business of the poet to drive the exiles to a decision about sovereignty because exiles do not want to choose; depressed people do not want to act, and despairing people think it does not matter. But the first step out of exile/despair is the clear embrace of a faithful sovereign and hence the press toward a decision.

First, Second Isaiah contrasts the two kinds of gods in an arrogant way. The one kind just wears you out:

> Bel bows down, Nebo stoops,
>   their idols are on beasts and cattle;
> these things you carry are loaded
>   as burdens on weary beasts. (Isa 46:1)

They must be carried around, and all an exile needs is more dead weight. Contrast this with God who in his freedom needs no exiles to carry him:

> Harken to me, O house of Jacob,
>   all the remnant of the house of Israel,
> who have been borne by me from your birth,
>   carried from the womb; . . .
> I have made, and I will bear;
>   I will carry and will save. (Isa 46:3-4; see 43:22-24)

If energy is what is in short supply, it is better to find a God who is free, able, and willing to take responsibility for his godness. There is high irony in a weary, despairing exile being in the image of a god who must be carried around because of fatigue. But the adherents of this other God are energized, empowered, and capable of living a faithful life. The contrast I have discerned is not new and has often been discerned, but what I do not want to miss is the socio-political dimension of the poem that adherence to the royal consciousness and its definition of reality make people weary and hopeless. It means nothing to recite such radical poetry unless we are clear about the battle for definition of reality that always lives close to the realities of power.

The contrast of the gods and the ridicule of the Babylonian gods is brought closer by a parallel ridicule of Madam Babylon. What kind of madam is Dame Babylon? A grand dame with courtly manner? A tyrannical old lady? A lady with a house like such a lady keeps? That is all over, for the new history of Israel with Yahweh means the end of this imperial history:

> Come down and sit in the dust,
>> O virgin daughter of Babylon;
> sit on the ground without a throne,
>> O daughter of the Chaldeans!
> For you shall no more be called
>> tender and delicate.
> Take the millstones and grind meal,
>> put off your veil,
> strip off your robe, uncover your legs,
>> pass through the rivers.
> Your nakedness shall be uncovered,
>> and your shame shall be seen. (Isa 47:1-3)

The poet engages in the kind of guerrilla warfare that is always necessary on behalf of oppressed people. First, the hated one must be ridiculed and made reachable, for then she may be disobeyed and seen as a nobody who claims no allegiance and keeps no promises. The big house yields no real life, need not be feared, cannot be trusted, and must not be honored.

When the Babylonian gods have been mocked, when the Babylonian culture has been ridiculed, and when the dethroned king is re-enthroned, then history is inverted. Funeral becomes festival, grief becomes doxology, and despair turns to amazement. Perhaps it is no more than a cultic event, but don't sell it short because cult kept close to historical experience can indeed energize people. For example, witness the African American churches and civil rights movements or the liberation resistance in Latin America. The cult may be a staging for the inversion that the kings think is not possible. It is the inversion that the grim royal middle class among us does not believe in, and it is the inversion that surprises people who are powerless. Inversions are not easy, not without cost, and never neat and clear. But we ought not underestimate the power of the poet. Inversions may begin in a change of language, a redefined perceptual field, or unaltered consciousness. So his poetry speaks about the inversion even in exile and the images tumble out. Three of them are of particular importance.

New Song

When the new king rules, it is new song time (Isa 42:10). It has always been new song time when the new king arrives and there is no more calling of the skilled mourners who know how to cry on call. The funeral is ended, for now it is festival time. It is time for the children and for all who can sing new songs and discern new situations. The old songs had to be sung in the presence of mockers (Ps 137:3). And they were an embarrassment because they spoke about all that had failed. But new song time is a way to sing a new social reality as the freedom songs stood behind every freedom act. The energy comes from the song that will sing Yahweh to his throne and Babylon to her grave. As Abraham Heschel has seen, only people in covenant can sing. New song time is when a new covenant inaugurates a new mode of reality.

Birth to the Barren

A second image is birth to the barren one. The notion of "barrenness" of course refers to a biological problem of having no children. It is clear, however, that the motif also is treated metaphorically, as in Isa 54:1-3, to refer to a loss of a future and therefore to hopelessness. Thus "barrenness" can refer to a variety of social circumstances; conversely, "birth" then comes to be taken metaphorically as the opening of a future and the generation of an alternative by the miraculous power of God. The notion of barrenness may be taken as a condition of despair in our society. Thus, for example, "eunuchs" of both genders have their manhood and womanhood taken away by the pressure and demand of the corporation, the academy, or the church. Indeed, it is clear that professors and pastors often have their energies and family lives taken from them just as effectively as corporate types. They have insufficient energy to bear or to beget, and who wants to birth new children for Babylon? Our history always begins with the barren, with Sarah (Gen 11:30), with Rebekah (Gen 25:21), with Rachel (Gen 29:31), with Hannah (1 Sam 1:2), and with Elizabeth (Luke 1:7). Among those, always as good as dead (Heb 11:12), the wondrous gift is given. The inability to bear is a curious thing, and we know that for all our science the reasons most often are historical, symbolic, and interpersonal. It is often news—good news, doxology—that brings the new future to effect and the new energy to birth.

So the inversion is the occasion for the poet to speak Israel into a new future:

> Sing, O barren one, who did not bear;
>> bring forth into singing and cry aloud,
>> you who have not been in travail!
> For the children of the desolate one will be more
>> than the children of her that is married, says the LORD.
>>> (Isa 54:1)

The oldest promises are again set in motion, and Babylon cannot stop them. Whenever the issues are set so that it is God's promises against Babylon, it is no contest. Babylon cannot stop the energizing of God. He will keep even the promises to mother Sarah.

Nourishment

A third image is that of nourishment. If you eat the bread of Babylon for very long, you will be destroyed. Some liked the bread of Babylon, and they became Babylonians; but Israelites who are exiles will not accommodate that imperial bread. So the poet in his statement about alternative bread dismantles the Babylonian bakery:

> Ho, every one who thirsts, come to the waters;
> and he who has no money,
>> come, . . . buy wine and milk
>> without money and without price.
> Why do you spend your money for that which is not bread,
>> and your labor for that which does not satisfy? (Isa 55:1-2)

By the time he has finished talking about bread he has in a deft move articulated the best Israelite promise (to David), the glory of Yahweh (at the expense of the Babylonian god Marduk), and homecoming:

> Incline your ear, and come to me;
>> hear, that your life may live;
> and I will make with you an everlasting covenant,
>> my steadfast sure love for David. (Isa 55:3)

Now let me admit that it is perfectly silly to talk about new songs, many births, and fresh bread. These are metaphors that do not seem to touch the reality of today's hardware and arsenal. Perhaps that is correct, but we must also observe that such items were silly the first time they were named in imperial, scientific Babylon. The hardware will not immediately surrender and the great kings will not readily abdicate power. Consider, for example, the wait through decades in the struggle against apartheid in South Africa and Nelson Mandela's twenty-six years in Robin Island Prison. The prophet seeks only to spark the imagination of this people, and that in itself turns despair to energy.

Second Isaiah gives his people a remarkable gift. He gives them back their faith by means of rearticulating the old story. He gives them the linguistic capacity to confront despair rather than be surrounded by it. And he creates new standing ground outside the dominant consciousness upon which new humanness is possible. A cynic might argue that nothing has really changed. And indeed, nothing really changed if only the fall of empires is anything and if it must happen immediately. But prophets are not magicians. Their art and calling are only with words that evoke alternatives, and reshaped hardware will not overcome despair in any case. That will come only with the recognition that life has not been fully consigned to us and that there is another who has reserved for himself his sovereign freedom from us and for us. He is at work apart from us and apart from Babylon. The godness of God takes the form of liberation for exiles. So Gerhard von Rad settled on that most remarkable of all texts that we should not speak until we decide if we trust it:

> Remember not the former things,
>   nor consider things of old.
> Behold, I am doing a new thing;
>   now it springs forth, do you not perceive it? (Isa 43:18-19)

Those not comforted can hardly believe such a thing can be uttered. But clearly they will have no personal joy, no public justice, no corporate repentance, and no family humaneness until the community receives a newness it cannot generate for itself.

A second majestic text, I believe, is pertinent to the fatigue among us, the fatigue from not deciding or from having settled for Babylon. First about the Lord:

> He does not faint or grow weary,
>> his understanding is unsearchable.
> He gives power to the faint,
>> and to him who has no might he increases strength.
>>> (Isa 40:28-29)

And then the promise to all of us exiles:

> Even youths shall faint and be weary,
>> and young men shall fall exhausted;
> but they who wait for the Lord shall renew their strength,
>> they shall mount up with wings like eagles,
> they shall run and not be weary,
>> they shall walk and not faint. (Isa 40:30-31)

The poet contrasts us in our waiting and in our going ahead. For those who take initiative into their own hands, either in the atheism of pride or in the atheism of despair, the words are weary, faint, and exhausted. The inverse comes with waiting: renewed strength, mounting up, running, and walking. But that is in waiting.[11] It is in receiving and not grasping, in inheriting and not possessing, in praising and not seizing. It is in knowing that initiative has passed from our hands and we are safer for it. Obviously this becomes more than a critique of Babylon. It is also a critique of every effort to reorganize on our own, and it is a warning about settling in any exile as home.

The newness from God is the only serious source of energy. And that energy for which people yearn is precisely what the royal consciousness—either of Solomon or Nebuchadnezzar—cannot give. The prophet must not underestimate his or her urgent calling, for the community of faith has no other source of newness. I am aware that this runs dangerously close to passivity, as trust often does, and that it stands at the brink of cheap grace, as grace must always do. But that risk must be run because exiles must always learn that our hope is never generated among us but always given to us. And whenever it is given we are amazed.

Jeremiah and Second Isaiah together, poets of pathos and amazement, speak in laments and doxologies. They cannot be torn from each other. Reading Jeremiah alone leaves faith in death where God finally will not stay. And reading Second Isaiah alone leads us to imagine that we may receive comfort without tears and tearing. Clearly, only those who anguish will sing new songs. Without anguish the new song is likely to be strident and just more royal fakery.

5

Criticism and Pathos
in Jesus of Nazareth

The dominant consciousness must be radically criticized and the
dominant community must be finally dismantled. The purpose
of an alternative community with an alternative consciousness is
for the sake of that criticism and dismantling. In considering the
work of Jeremiah, I have argued that the royal culture of his time
was numbed and therefore unable to face any drastic historical
ending, and that the only way to penetrate that numbed consciousness of denial was by the public presentation of grief. In his
poetry of grief, Jeremiah tried to bring Israel to a sense of the end
of a social world that the royal apparatus tried its best to perpetuate. If we are to understand prophetic criticism, we must see that
its characteristic idiom is anguish and not anger. The point of the
idiom is to permit the community to engage its own anguish,
which it prefers to deny. Such a judgment about the way of prophetic criticism suggests that the prophets were keenly aware of
how change is effected and were remarkably sensitive to the
characteristic ways of openness and resistance.

In this chapter we shall consider how the prophetic ministry
of criticism is related to Jesus of Nazareth. Clearly Jesus cannot
be understood simply as prophet, for that designation, like every
other, is inadequate for the historical reality of Jesus. Nonetheless, among his other functions it is clear that Jesus functioned as
a prophet. In both his teaching and his very presence, Jesus of

Nazareth presented the ultimate criticism of the royal consciousness. He has, in fact, dismantled the dominant culture and nullified its claims. The way of his ultimate criticism is his decisive
solidarity with marginal people and the accompanying vulnera-
bility required by that solidarity. The only solidarity worth
affirming is solidarity characterized by the same helplessness
they know and experience. So now I review several dimensions
of that ultimate criticism.

Jesus' Birth

The birth of Jesus itself represents a decisive criticism of the
dominant consciousness. The Lucan account of his solidarity
with the poor and the Matthean presentation of his abrasive conflict with the powers that be (seen in the birth narratives) both
point to the emergence of an alternative consciousness. No
attempt, of course, needs to be made to harmonize the two ver-
sions as they move in different directions for different reasons
and make different affirmations. Nevertheless, in completed
form they are perfectly complementary in dismantling by criticism and in energizing by amazement.

   The Gospel of Matthew. The dismantling in the
Matthean version is found in Matt 2:16-23. The episode juxta-
poses *the destructive rage of the pseudo-king* (v. 16) and *the grief of
the prophetic tradition* (v. 17). The rage of Herod is presented as
the last gasp of the old order and the desperate attempt to hold on
to the old way.

   As in ancient Israel, it is characteristic of kings to deny the
end of the old order and, in their blindness, to take any steps to
perpetuate what has in fact already ended. Thus Herod engages
in self-deception and denial using his best talents, but they are
not enough because the king cannot stop the end. In contrast to
this is the pathos of Rachel, seen in Jeremiah. The raging of the
king comes to an end in grief and lamentation. It is the work of

the prophetic tradition to grieve the end, the very end the king cannot face, cannot stop, and surely cannot grieve.

In the construction of Matthew 1, vv. 16-17 on king and prophet are preliminary, whereas vv. 18-23 carry the action. The contrast is complete: the king is dead and the angel brings the child to his future. Herod has clearly been outdone; he is no real king. Jesus is the real king (2:11), and the real king stands as a decisive negation of the no-king. The grieving of Rachel is a grieving for the ending that the king seemed to manage but that in the end undid the king. Indeed, the grieving of Rachel concerns both the ultimate criticism and the newness about to emerge from the criticism. That Jesus is presented as the alternative is signaled in vv. 22-23.[1] He is a Nazarene, which is to say surely a marginal, faithful one. He is marginal geographically (as a Galilean from *Nazareth*; vv. 22-23a); and he is also religiously marginal (as a *Nazarite*, that is, a consecrated one; see Num 6:1-21) embodying a poignant counter-reality—reality always to contrast and finally to destroy the dominant reality.

The Gospel of Luke. In parallel fashion, the Lucan account of the disclosure to the shepherds, the representative marginal ones, announces a newness that will displace the old regime. Appropriately the recipients of unexpected newness are filled with wonder and awe (Luke 2:17-20). The intrusion embodied in the birth of Jesus causes a radical inversion:

> He has scattered the proud in the imagination of their hearts,
> he has put down the mighty from their thrones,
>   and exalted those of low degree;
> he has filled the hungry with good things,
>   and the rich he has sent empty away. (Luke 1:51-53)[2]

The birth of Jesus brings a harsh end to a Herodian reality that seemed ordained forever, and it created a new historical situation for marginal people that none in their despair could have anticipated. While the Lucan version celebrates the emerging newness, the Matthean version places grief at the center of the narrative. The newness does not come without anguish, pain, and tears. The tears are for the last desperate destructiveness by the king to save himself. And they are for the victims of that ending because the king will not die alone; he will take with him those he can who appear to be the ones who threaten him. The beginning in Jesus does not come without harsh ending, for that which is ending never ends graciously.

The Announcement of the Kingdom

Herod had reasoned correctly. The coming of Jesus meant the abrupt end of things as they were. Two texts are commonly cited as programmatic for the preaching of Jesus. In Mark 1:15 he announces the coming of the kingdom. But surely implicit in the announcement is the counterpart that present kingdoms will end and be displaced. In Luke 4:18-19 he announces that a new age was beginning, but that announcement carries within it a harsh criticism of all those powers and agents of the present order.[3] His message was to the poor, but others kept them poor and benefited from their poverty. He addressed the captives (which means bonded slaves), but others surely wanted that arrangement unchanged. He named the oppressed, but there are never oppressed without oppressors.

His ministry carried out the threat implicit in these two fundamental announcements. The ministry of Jesus is, of course, criticism that leads to radical dismantling. And as is characteristic, the guardians and profiteers of the present stability are acutely sensitive to any change that may question or challenge the present arrangement. Very early Jesus is correctly perceived as a clear and present danger to that order, and this is the problem with the promissory newness of the gospel: it never promises without threatening, it never begins without ending something, it never gives gifts without also assessing harsh costs. Jesus' radical criticism may be summarized in several representative actions.

Forgiveness. Jesus' readiness to forgive sin (Mark 2:1-11), which evoked amazement (v. 12), also appeared to be blasphemy, that is to say, a threat to the present religious sanctions. At one level the danger is that Jesus stood in the role of God (v. 7) and therefore claimed too much; but we should not miss the radical criticism of society contained in the act. Hannah Arendt had discerned that this was Jesus' most endangering action because if a society does not have an apparatus for forgiveness, then its members are fated to live forever with the consequences of any violation.[4] Thus the refusal to forgive sin (or the management of the machinery of forgiveness) amounts to enormous social control. While the claim of Jesus may have been religiously staggering, its threat to the forms of accepted social control was even greater.

Sabbath. Jesus' ability to heal and his readiness to do it on the Sabbath (Mark 3:1-6) evoked a conspiracy to kill him (v. 6). The violation is concerned not with the healing but with the Sabbath. Already in Mark 2:23-28 he has raised the issue, and obviously Jesus' understanding of the Sabbath is that it had become a way of enslavement. Predictably, the objection comes from those who managed the Sabbath and benefited from it. The Sabbath thus stood as the sacred sign of a social settlement, and to call that special day into question unsettled the entire settlement. The day that came to articulate social order was now transformed into an occasion for freedom, freedom that rejected the settlement.[5]

Table fellowship. Jesus was willing to eat with outcasts (Mark 2:15-17), which threatened the fundamental morality of society. The outcasts were the product of a legal arrangement that determined what was acceptable and unacceptable, clean and unclean, right and wrong. Crossing over the barrier of right and wrong implied that in the dispensing of mercy the wrong were as entitled as were the right, and therefore all meaningful distinctions were obliterated.

Healing and Exorcism. Further distinctive aspects of Jesus' prophetic ministry are his healings and exorcisms. He touched those afflicted with illness, loss, torment, and demonic possession; and he addressed both the personal and communal aspects of these experiences. These are radical acts because they cross boundaries—including rather than excluding—fearlessly reaching out to those deemed unclean by society (Mark 7:24-30), sinners (Mark 2:1-12), and under God's judgment (John 9:1). Note the important connection between these stories and those about the prophets Elijah and Elisha (1 Kings 17—2 Kings 10). Like the gospel stories, the accounts of Elijah and Elisha were told in the context of conflict in political-religion, the abuse of royal power, and the disenfranchisement of the peasants. The political import of Jesus exorcizing the Gerasene's demons called "Legion," for example, would not be missed by villagers living in land controlled by Rome's troops (Mark 5:1-13).[6] All these actions are signs of God's reign breaking through (Matt 4:23; Luke 7:18-23).

Women. Jesus' association in public with women who were not his kin was a scandalous breech of decorum and a challenge to the gender boundaries of the first century. He let a socially outcast woman touch him (Luke 7:36-50). He spoke with the Samaritan woman at the well (John 4:1-26). He healed a woman with a flow of blood (Mark 5:25-34). And women traveled with him around Galilee and then to Jerusalem (Mark 15:40-41). Jesus' proclamation of God's reign and the attendant healing, eating, and community-building was not to be only a male enterprise, but an inclusive one.[7]

Taxes and Debt. Jesus often refers to debt in the gospels. Connected with this, the day-laborers were likely peasants who had lost their land due to heavy taxation (Matt 20:1-16). One of the petitions of the Lord's Prayer specifically mentions reciprocal debt forgiveness (Matt 6:12; Luke 11:4), and this was not likely metaphorical. And Jesus' enigmatic saying about paying taxes

(Mark 12:13-17; Luke 20:26) was at least open to the interpreta-tion that he was a tax resister (Luke 23:2). The reason for Jesus speaking out about these issues of political-economy was the weight of taxes, tithes, tolls, rents, and confiscation on the peas-ants of Galilee and Judea.[8]

Temple. Jesus' attitude toward the temple (Mark 11:15-19; John 2:18-22) was finally the most ominous threat because there he spoke directly about the destruction. In so doing he of course voiced the intent of the enemies of the church and of the state. Moreover, in his speech about the temple he quotes from the temple sermon of Jeremiah (Jer 7:11), thereby mobilizing that painful memory of dismantling criticism and in fact radically replicating it here.[9] In critiquing the temple, Jesus struck at the center of the doctrine of election, which can be traced in the Zion tradition at least as far back as Isaiah and which assumed a guar-anteed historical existence for this special people gathered around this special shrine. Thus Jesus advances the critical tradition of Jeremiah against the royal tradition reflected in Isaiah.[10]

All these actions, together with Jesus' other violations of social convention, are a heavy criticism of the "righteousness of the law." The law had become in his day a way for the managers of society, religious even more than civil, to effectively control not only moral-ity but the political-economic valuing that lay behind the morality. Thus his criticism of the "law" is not to be dismissed as an attack on "legalism" in any moralistic sense, as is sometimes done in reductionist Pauline interpretation. Rather, his critique concerns the fundamental social valuing of his society. In practice Jesus has seen, as Marx later made clear, that the law can be a social conven-tion to protect the current distribution of economic and political power.[11] Jesus, in the tradition of Jeremiah, dared to articulate the end of a consciousness that could not keep its promises but that in fact denied the very humanness it purported to give. As is always the case, it is a close call to determine if in fact Jesus caused the dismantling or if he voiced what was indeed about to happen in any case. But Jesus, along with the other prophets, is regularly treated as though giving voice is causing the dismantling. And indeed, in such a consciousness that may be the reality.

We may note in passing that in the temple-cleansing narrative as well as in the Matthean birth narrative it is the Jeremiah tradition that is mentioned. Moreover, in the Matthean version of eating with sinners (Matt 9:10-13), as well as in working on the Sabbath (Matt 12:5-6), the appeal is to Hos 6:6. It is certainly important that appeal is made precisely to the most radical and anguished prophets of the dismantling.

Compassion

Jesus in his solidarity with the marginal ones is *moved to compassion*. Compassion constitutes a radical form of criticism, for it announces that the hurt is to be taken seriously, that the hurt is not to be accepted as normal and natural but is an abnormal and unacceptable condition for humanness. In the arrangement of "lawfulness" in Jesus' time, as in the ancient empire of Pharaoh, the one unpermitted quality of relation was compassion. Empires are never built or maintained on the basis of compassion. The norms of law (social control) are never accommodated to persons, but persons are accommodated to the norms. Otherwise the norms will collapse and with them the whole power arrangement. Thus the compassion of Jesus is to be understood not simply as a personal emotional reaction but as a public criticism in which he dares to act upon his concern against the entire numbness of his social context. Empires live by numbness. Empires, in their militarism, expect numbness about the human cost of war. Corporate economies expect blindness to the cost in terms of poverty and exploitation. Governments and societies of domination go to great lengths to keep the numbness intact. Jesus penetrates the numbness by his compassion and with his compassion takes the first step by making visible the odd abnormality that had become business as usual. Thus compassion that might be seen simply as generous goodwill is in fact criticism of the system, forces, and ideologies that produce the hurt. Jesus enters into the hurt and finally comes to embody it.

The characteristic Greek word for compassion, *splagchnoisomai,* means to let one's innards embrace the feeling or situation of another.[12] Thus Jesus embodies the hurt that the marginal ones know by taking it into his own person and his own history. Their hurt came from being declared outside the realm of the normal, and Jesus engages with them in a situation of abnormality. Concretely, his criticism as embodied hurt is expressed toward the sick: "As he went ashore he saw a great throng; and he had *compassion* on them, and healed them" (Matt 14:14). And toward the hungry:

> As he went ashore he saw a great throng, and he had compassion on them because they were like sheep without a shepherd; and he began to teach them many things. (Mark 6:34)
>
> "I have compassion on the crowd because they have been with me now three days, and have nothing to eat." (Mark 8:2)

And toward the one who grieved the dead:

> And as he drew near to the gate of the city, behold, a man who had died was being carried out, the only son of his mother, and she was a widow; and a large crowd from the city was with her. And when the Lord saw her, he had compassion on her. (Luke 7:12-13)

More programmatically, his compassion is for the whole range of human persons who are harassed and helpless:

> And Jesus went about all the cities and villages, teaching in their synagogues and preaching the gospel of the kingdom, and healing every disease and every infirmity. When he saw the crowds, he had *compassion* for them because they were harassed and helpless, like sheep without a shepherd. (Matt 9:35-36)

Matthew has taken the saying that Mark has in the setting of the feeding and made it a more general statement, both by placing it at a narrative transition and by inserting the words "harassed and helpless." Those words are polemical, for the people did not get helpless by themselves but were rendered helpless. And to speak of harassment is to suggest that some others are doing the harassing. Thus the Matthean version is much more direct and critical. Moreover, the Matthean saying has attending it a harsh judgment statement: "The harvest is plentiful, but the laborers are few; pray therefore the Lord of the harvest to send out laborers into his harvest" (Matt 9:37-38). The image of harvest clearly is one of dismantling judgment. The juxtaposition of "harvest" with "helpless and harassed" puts the present ordering and its managers on notice.

Again we may note the appeal to the radical prophetic tradition. The internalization of hurt for the marginal ones is especially faithful to the tradition of anguish in Hosea and Jeremiah. In Hosea the internalization of hurt is especially clear in 11:8-9: "My heart recoils within me, my compassion (*reḥem*) grows warm and tender." The same internalization is evident in Jeremiah as I have presented it. Both prophets and now Jesus after them bring to expression and embodiment all the hurt, human pain, and grief that the dominant royal culture has tried so hard to repress, deny, and cover over.

It is instructive that in the teaching of Jesus it is precisely his two best-known parables that contain the word under discussion. First, in the narrative of the good Samaritan it is the Samaritan who has compassion (Luke 10:33).[13] Second, in the story of the prodigal son, it is precisely the father who has compassion (Luke 15:20). Clearly the key person in each of these parables embodies the alternative consciousness from which the dominant consciousness is criticized. Both the Samaritan and the father are Jesus' peculiar articulation against the dominant culture, and so they stand as a radical threat. The Samaritan by his action judges the dominant way by disregard of the marginal. The ones who pass by, obviously carriers of the dominant tradition, are numbed, indifferent, and do not notice. The Samaritan expresses a new way that displaces the old arrangements in which outcasts are simply out. The replacing of numbness with compassion, that is, the end of cynical indifference and the beginning of noticed pain, signals a social revolution. In similar fashion, the father, by his ready embrace of his unacceptable son, condemns the "righteousness of the law" by which society is currently ordered and by which social rejects are forever rejected. Thus the stories, if seen as radical dismantling criticism, bring together *the internalization of pain* and *external transformation*. The capacity to feel the hurt of the marginal people means an end to all social arrangements that nullified pain by a remarkable depth of numbness.

Jesus is remembered and presented by the early church as the faithful embodiment of an alternative consciousness. In his compassion, he embodies the anguish of those rejected by the dominant culture, and as embodied anguish, he has the authority to show the deathly end of the dominant culture. Quite clearly, the one thing the dominant culture cannot tolerate or co-opt is compassion, the ability to stand in solidarity with the victims of the present order. It can manage charity and good intentions, but it has no way to resist solidarity with pain or grief. So the structures of competence and competition stand helpless before the one who groaned the groans of those who are hurting. And in their groans they announce the end of the dominant social world. The imperial consciousness lives by its capacity to still the groans and to go on with business as usual as though none were hurting and there were no groans. If the groans become audible, if they can be heard in the streets and markets and courts, then the consciousness of domination is already jeopardized. Thus the groans in Egypt heralded the social innovation (Exod 2:23-25; 3:7). In like manner, Jesus had the capacity to give voice to the very hurt that had been muted, and therefore newness could break through. Newness comes precisely from expressed pain.[14] Suffering made audible and visible produces hope, articulated grief is the gate of newness, and the history of Jesus is the history of entering into the pain and giving it voice.

Jesus' radical criticism as embodied anguish is evident in two other places where his grief is unmistakable. They probably should be seen together. First, in the narrative of the death of Lazarus, Jesus is presented as the powerful healer who can bring life from death (John 11:1-57). That is the main thrust of the narrative, but that central act recounted in v. 44 is enveloped by two others. First the power of Jesus is evidenced in the context of his grief:

> When Jesus saw her weeping, and the Jews who came with her also weeping, he was deeply moved in spirit and troubled; and he said, "Where have you laid him?" They said to him, "Lord, come and see." Jesus wept. (John 11:33-35)

He is not the majestic, unmoved Lord but rather the one with the passion who knows and shares in the anguish of the brother and sister. The fact that Jesus weeps and that he is moved in spirit and troubled contrasts remarkably with the dominant culture. That is not the way of power, and it is scarcely the way among those who intend to maintain firm social control. But in this scene Jesus is engaged not in social control but in dismantling the power of death, and he does so by submitting himself to the pain and grief present in the situation, the very pain and grief that the dominant society must deny.

We may digress to comment on the other, quite unrelated Lazarus story in Luke 16:19-31. Lazarus is presented as the radical contrast to the rich man. The contrast among other things contrasts the *numbness* of the rich man with the *pain* of Lazarus:

> There was a rich man, who was clothed in purple and fine linen and who feasted sumptuously every day. At his gate lay a poor man named Lazarus, full of sores, who desired to be fed; . . . the dogs came and licked his sores. (Luke 16:19-21)

The contrast surely operates at many levels. But among other things, the narrative suggests that the rich man who is numbed by his possessions and social status has no future; there is nothing but an end for him. By contrast, the poor man Lazarus, unencumbered either by possessions or by social status, is beset by grief and pain. And, says Jesus, this is the bearer of the future. The contrast, in the context of our discussion, concerns the *numbed one* who knows no future except more of the present and *the suffering one* who receives newness from the Father.

In the Johannine story of the raising of Lazarus, we have noted Jesus' deep compassion in which he shares the grief of the others. We have also noted his powerful action to bring life, an action that seems conditioned by his capacity to enter the grief. The other factor to be noted is that his capacity to invert evokes immediate and sharp hostility from the governors of the old order:

> So the chief priests and Pharisees gathered the council, and said, "What are we to do? For this man performs many signs." . . . Now the chief priests and the Pharisees had given orders that if anyone knew where he was, he should let them know, so that they might arrest him. (John 11:47, 57)

Jesus gives signs; he promises alternatives; he suggests newness. His promise represents a correctly perceived threat to the old order. Jesus brings newness in the situation but only in his grief. It is not psychologizing but integral to the narrative that grief, embodied anguish, is the route to newness. The old order that does not want newness keeps it from coming by denying the grief. Where grief for the death of the old order is not faced and embodied and expressed, the old order must go on a while longer, dead though it is.

The other act of decisive weeping, to be linked to this act of passion and power, is Jesus' weeping over Jerusalem:

> And when he drew near and saw the city he wept over it, saying, "Would that even today you knew the things that make for peace! But now they are hid from your eyes." (Luke 19:41-42)

Here the weeping is over Jerusalem, beloved city of God. Jesus' weeping over Jerusalem, like his weeping over Lazarus, is a sharing in an anguish unto death. The difference is that everyone knew Lazarus was dead, and Jesus raised him to new life. The grieving was finished for Lazarus, whereas everyone thought Jerusalem was alive, and he grieved the death of the city. The grief over the city is ironic because Jerusalem is the main sponsor of numbness and lives itself in denial of grief. Indeed, the governors in Jerusalem want especially to keep the grieving from happening because they cannot and do not wish to acknowledge the end. The grief of Jesus, like the grief of Jeremiah (notice that Luke 19:43 is reminiscent of Jer 6:6), is that this center of promise is now ended and bankrupt. And so the words of Jesus describe the destruction. In the Matthean counterpart, the grief over Jerusalem is preceded by a series of woes (Matt 23:13-33); but woes serve the same purpose, announcing a grieving over death.[15]

The compassion of Jesus has two sides. On the one hand, it is a frontal attack upon the dominant culture. He grieves over the death of the old world and the old city even when most did not know it was dead. His criticism is not in anger but in pathos, for none loved the city more. Nonetheless, he knew about the deathly conflict between his own mission and the dominant culture of Jerusalem, for he understood early that he must die at the hands of Jerusalem.

Jesus' compassion is not only criticism of what is deathly, for in his criticism and solidarity he evidences power to transform. So his embrace of the death his people are dying leads to a restored Lazarus, to healed people, to fed crowds, to a cared-for man, to an accepted son, and to good news for the harassed and helpless. The heavy criticism of Jesus holds the offer and possibility of an alternative beginning.

Jesus' Crucifixion

It is the crucifixion of Jesus that is the decisive criticism of the royal consciousness. The crucifixion of Jesus is not to be understood simply in good liberal fashion as the sacrifice of a noble man, nor should we too quickly assign a cultic, priestly theory of atonement to the event. Rather, we might see in the crucifixion of Jesus the ultimate act of prophetic criticism in which Jesus announces the end of a world of death (the same announcement as that of Jeremiah) and takes the death into his own person. Therefore we say that the ultimate criticism is that God embraces the death that God's people must die.[16] The criticism consists not in standing over against but in standing with; the ultimate criticism is not one of triumphant indignation but one of the passion and compassion that completely and irresistibly undermine the world of competence and competition. The contrast is stark and total: this *passionate* man set in the midst of *numbed* Jerusalem. And only the *passion* can finally penetrate the *numbness*.

Passion Announcements. The radical criticism embodied in the crucifixion can be discerned in the "passion announcements" of Mark's Gospel:

> And he began to teach them that the Son of man must suffer many things, and be rejected by the elders and the chief priests and the scribes, and be killed, and after three days rise again. (Mark 8:31)
>
> "The Son of man will be delivered into the hands of men, and they will kill him; and when he is killed, after three days he will rise." (9:31)
>
> "Behold, we are going up to Jerusalem; and the Son of man will be delivered to the chief priests and the scribes, and they will condemn him to death, and deliver him to the Gentiles; and they will mock him, and spit upon him, and scourge him, and kill him; and after three days he will rise." (10:33-34)

There is no more radical criticism than these statements, for they announce that the power of God takes the form of death and that real well-being and victory only appear via death. So the sayings dismantle the dominant theories of power by asserting that all such would-be power is in fact no-power. Thus the passion announcements of Jesus are the decisive dismissal of every self-serving form of power upon which the royal consciousness is based. Just that formula, *Son of man* must *suffer*—Son of man/

suffer!—is more than the world can tolerate, for the phrase of ultimate power, "Son of man," has as its predicate the passion to death. It is true that no precise counterpart can be found in the history of Moses. Moses never speaks or acts in this way; but we may pause to discern important continuities between the two. Moses also dismantled the empire and declared it to be a no-power (remember Exod 8:18) by disregarding the claims of the imperial reality and trusting fully in the Lord of justice and freedom. In parallel fashion, the dominant power is dismantled by appeal to an uncredentialed God.

That the passion sayings of Jesus constitute the ultimate criticism of the royal consciousness is evident in the reaction of the faithful. *First,* Peter, on behalf of the church, rejects the criticism as too radical and he is roundly reprimanded (Mark 8:32-33). *Second,* the disciples did not understand and are afraid to ask (9:32). *Third,* they respond, indicating they understood nothing, by fresh dispute about their own power and authority (10:35-37). The criticism of Jesus is too radical, not only for the imperial managers but also for his own followers. None of us is prepared for such decisive criticism.

Sayings on the Cross. Jesus' sayings on the cross as preserved in the various traditions are the voice of an alternative consciousness. His initial plea for forgiveness for his enemies is an act of criticism (Luke 23:34), for it asserts the insanity of the dominant culture. On behalf of that world that has now sentenced him, he enters *a plea of temporary insanity.* A reference should be made here to the insightful interpretation of Paul Lehmann, who shows that the trial of Jesus before Pilate in fact has Pilate, and not Jesus, on trial.[17] The cry of Jesus from the cross, then, may be regarded as a decision (by the Judge) that the defendant (the old order) may not be punished because it is insane.

Second, his cry of despair is *an announcement of abandonment* (Mark 15:34). The whole known network of meaning has collapsed and a new, dangerous situation of faith has emerged.[18]

Thus Jesus experiences the result of the criticism; the old assurances and awarenesses of meaning are now all gone.[19]

Third, the ultimate criticism ends in *submission* (Luke 23:46), the last thing possible in a world of competence and control. Thus in that very world of control Jesus presents a new way of faithfulness that completely subverts the dominant way.

And finally, his assertion of paradise is a speech about the delegitimization of the world that killed him (Luke 23:43). Now he speaks from *a very different value system*. The very one called criminal is now welcomed to paradise; the outcast is the welcomed one. Jesus' new way of acting and speaking announces that another way is now operating. It is the final assertion that the old way is null and void.

Too much should not be made of these isolated statements of the cross, for each has its own complex development in the history of the tradition, which is undoubtedly in part a history of the liturgy. Nonetheless, together they form a statement that completely refutes the claims of those who seem to be in charge. These statements (a plea of insanity, a cry of abandonment, a groan of submission, and an assertion of a new way of graciousness) are a refutation of the world now brought to an end. The old order may be characterized as madness masquerading as control; phony assurance of sustained well-being; a desperate attempt to control and not submit; and a grim system of retribution. Thus each statement of Jesus is a counter-possibility that places all the old ways in question. The passion narrative of Jesus provides ground for prophetic criticism. It hints at a fresh way for the repentance of Lent.

Christological Hymn. This theological tradition of life in the shape of death and of power in the form of suffering is more than the dominant culture can receive or accept. That alternative discernment is evident in the theology of the cross both as narrated by Mark and as articulated by Paul. While many texts might be cited, here I mention the ancient hymn utilized by Paul:

Christ Jesus,
who though he was in the form of God,
   did not count equality with God
   a thing to be grasped,

but emptied himself,
   taking the form of a servant,
   being born in the likeness of men.

And being found in human form
   he humbled himself
   and became obedient unto death,
   even death on a cross.

Therefore God has highly exalted him
   and bestowed on him the name
   which is above every name,

that at the name of Jesus
   every knee should bow,
   in heaven and on earth and under the earth,

and every tongue confess
   that Jesus Christ is Lord,
   to the glory of God the father. (Phil 2:5-11)[20]

That tradition of radical criticism is about the self-giving emptiness of Jesus, about dominion through the loss of dominion, and about fullness coming only by self-emptying. The emptying is not to be related to self-negating meditation, for it is a thoroughly political image concerned with the willing surrender of power; it is the very thing kings cannot do and yet remain kings. Thus the entire royal self-understanding is refuted. The empty one who willingly surrendered power for obedience is the ultimately powerful one who can permit humanness where no other has authority to do so.

The Politics of Justice and Compassion

The crucifixion, then, is not an odd event in the history of faith, although it is the decisive event. It is, rather, the full expression of dismantling that has been practiced and insisted upon in the prophetic tradition since Moses confronted Pharaoh. As with Moses, so Jesus' ministry and death opposed the politics of oppression with the politics of justice and compassion. As with Moses, so Jesus' ministry and death contradicted the religion of God's captivity with the freedom of God to bring life where he will, even in the face of death.

The cross is the ultimate metaphor of prophetic criticism because it means the end of the old consciousness that brings death on everyone. The crucifixion articulates God's odd freedom, his strange justice, and his peculiar power. It is this *freedom* (read religion of God's freedom), *justice* (read economics of sharing), and *power* (read politics of justice) that break the power of the old age and bring it to death. Without the cross, prophetic imagination will likely be as strident and as destructive as that which it criticizes. The cross is the assurance that effective prophetic criticism is done not by an outsider but always by one who must embrace the grief, enter into the death, and know the pain of the criticized one.

Prophetic criticism aims to create an alternative consciousness with its own rhetoric and field of perception. That alternative consciousness, unless the criticism is to be superficial and external, has to do with the cross. Douglas John Hall has explored how we might think about this, suggesting that creative criticism must be ethically pertinent and premised on our own embrace of negativity.[21] This kind of prophetic criticism does not lightly offer alternatives, does not mouth assurances, and does not provide redemptive social policy. It knows that only those who mourn can be comforted, and so it first asks about how to mourn seriously and faithfully for the world passing away. Jesus understood and embodied that anguish Jeremiah felt so poignantly.

6

Energizing and Amazement in Jesus of Nazareth

The formation of an alternative community with an alternative consciousness is so that the dominant community may be criticized and finally dismantled. But more than dismantling, the purpose of the alternative community is to enable a new human beginning to be made. The primary work of Moses was to make a new human beginning with the religion of God's freedom and the politics of justice and compassion.

In considering the work of Second Isaiah, we have seen first that his forsaken community of exiles was in despair because it did not know or believe that any new beginning was possible and, second, that the only way to overcome the despair was the public presentation of hope. As the pre-exilic community was encapsulated in numbness, so the exilic community was beset by despair. As the pre-exilic prophet (Jeremiah) penetrated the numbness by the public presentation of grief, so the exilic prophet (Second Isaiah) penetrated the despair by the public presentation of hope. As Jeremiah presented grief as the ultimate criticism, so Second Isaiah brought Israel to a sense of a new historical beginning by the action of God in his sovereign and gracious freedom. If we are to understand prophetic energizing, we must see that its characteristic idiom is hope and not optimism.[1] The point of this idiom is to permit the community to engage in amazement that will not be prevented by the despair of the community for whom everything has collapsed.

When in the prophetic tradition we come to speak of the ultimate presentation of energy, we finally must turn to Jesus of Nazareth. We have seen that, by his actions and words, and especially by his crucifixion, he engaged in the dismantling of the royal consciousness and brought his community to face its grief in that dismantling. The counterpart to that, and indeed the focus of the work of Jesus, was not dismantling but the inauguration of a new thing. This imagination and action stood against all the discerned data and in the face of the doubt and resistance of those to whom he came. That ultimate energizing gave people a future when they believed that the grim present was the end and the only possible state of existence. That new future in which no one believed was born in staggering amazement, for it was correctly perceived as underived and unextrapolated and therefore beyond human understanding (Phil 4:7) and human control.

It is the task of every would-be prophet to present such underived and unextrapolated newness. It is the claim of every would-be prophet that the newness is possible only because God is God, and God is faithful to the promised newness. So the argument of this chapter is simply that Jesus of Nazareth is the fulfillment and quintessence of the prophetic tradition. He brought to public expression the newness given by God. The response to his work and person is amazement, for it is amazing that anything should be unextrapolated in our history. That amazement gave energy, the only kind of energy that gives newness.

Jesus' Birth

The birth of Jesus is presented, especially by Luke, as decisive energizing toward a new social reality. The early church obviously struggled with how to begin its tale of Jesus. The beginning must be just right, for there is something new here that can scarcely be articulated, and the articulation must match the reality of the newness. The birth itself is presented by the song of the angels against the rulers of the day. The rulers had decreed a census and all the managing ways that went with it, but a census never led to energy or newness.[2] This new one from God could not and would not be counted. The grim holding action of census was penetrated by the unscheduled and unextrapolated song of angels who sing a new song for a new king. There is no way to begin this new narrative except by a new song in the mouth of angels, authorized from the throne of God. The very idiom of lyric means the penetration of closed royal prose. The beginning is with a *song* that stands in conflict with the *decree*. All the old history is by decree, but the new history begins another way. The birth of a new king marks a new beginning in heaven and on earth of a very different kind. So the Lucan version is in keeping with the devices of Second Isaiah, an enthronement formula and a new song for a new king. The birth of the new king, the one Rome did not anticipate and Herod could not stop, begins another history, which carries in it the end of all old royal histories. Characteristically, the birth of this new king marks a jubilee from old debts, an amnesty from old crimes, and a beginning again in a movement of freedom (so Luke 4:18-19).

The newly lyrical beginning is received by the only ones who could receive it, the shepherds, who were certainly bearers of society's marginality. There is no hint here of the lyrics being heard by any of the managers of the census. They just kept counting and assuming that all numbers come in sequence and finally add up. This beginning is not among those who operate the old order; rather, it emerges among the victims of the old order. It comes among a barren old woman (Elizabeth), an innocent but believing young woman (Mary), an old man struck dumb (Zechariah), and society's rejects (shepherds). It is a place for amazement because they are the ones who had known the depths of grief. Thus amazement happened among them and not among those who had not yet grieved the death of the old age.

The newness announced and observed is not a newness that fits the old categories, for it is precisely the old categories that are now shattered. So there is no easy categorizing of the event, as kings are inclined to do. The event will not be contained by the rationality of the king, ancient or contemporary. Rather, there is here a brooding, a wondering, and an amazement. The shepherds themselves are moved to a doxology (Luke 2:20), Mary is left with pondering (2:19), and the others are left in amazement (2:18). The praise, brooding, and astonishment are appropriate to the event, for it was not expected and it could not be understood on any conventional grounds. There is criticism here, for implicitly the old rulers are dismantled and have no access to the new future. A newness has begun, and it is a newness to the victimized ones. Invited to join are all those who have groaned under the ways of the old kings.

The same energizing power from the birth is evident in the poems and songs with which the Lucan birth narrative is surrounded. The songs are about promises being kept just when all the promises appear to have failed. This is the character of the energy in the gospel; apparently failed promises are being kept just when we thought they were abandoned. So the song of Mary (the Magnificat; Luke 1:46-55) is about the unthinkable turn in human destinies when all seemed impossible: "For with God nothing will be impossible" (v. 37). The answering song of Zechariah (1:68-79) is a song of new possibilities given late, but not too late, possibilities of deliverance/forgiveness/mercy/light/peace. The old order had left nothing but enslavement/guilt/judgment/darkness and hostility, and no one could see how that could ever change. It will not be explained but only sung about, for the song penetrates royal reason. The song releases energy that the king can neither generate nor prevent. The transformation is unmistakable. Tongues long dumb in hopelessness could sing again.[3] The newness wrought by Jesus will not be explained, for to explain is to force it into old royal categories. And in any case the energizing hope comes precisely to those ill-schooled in explanation and understandings. It comes to those who will settle for amazements they can neither explain nor understand.

Jesus' Ministry

The ministry of Jesus is, of course, the energizing that leads to the radical beginnings precisely when none seemed possible. Everything hinges on the ministry and the narrative rushes to the ministry. Indeed, the birth narratives are told only because of the impact of Jesus' ministry. The birth is only a hope; but the ministry is where the possibilities of hope must seriously engage the world of despair. Jesus is presented and trusted as the one whose very person made a difference. His words and acts were not without abrasion, but those who were open and received, who let gifts be given and reality be redefined, did not notice the abrasion. Indeed, it was not an abrasion to them, for the abrasion was against the old order whose death they had long since faced and affirmed.

What people noticed is that life had been strangely and inexplicably changed. The change did not come by proper means, for Jesus' *means* were as much in violation of proper order as *the results* violated rationality. (Means, like ends, are a scandal.) The strange newness happened in ways that did not wait for royal sanction, and they did not happen in any of the ways that administered things happen.

Luke is especially aware that Jesus' deeds took place among the marginal victims of society. Mark is more sensitive to the fact that hardness of heart can stop his work, indeed, that where there is no belief he could not energize (Mark 6:5-6). It was possible to resist the new energizing, but there were great numbers who were free to embrace it and had no need to resist. The whole movement is summarized in staggering simplicity:

> The blind receive their sight, the lame walk, lepers are cleansed, and the deaf hear, the dead are raised up, the poor have good news preached to them. (Luke 7:22)

And then the response. Of course, those who valued what is old resisted:

The chief priests and the scribes and the principal men of the people sought to destroy him. (Luke 19:47)

The Pharisees went out, and immediately held counsel with the Herodians against him, how to destroy him. (Mark 3:6)

And the scribes who came down from Jerusalem said, "He is possessed by Beelzebul, and by the prince of demons he casts out the demons." (Mark 3:22)

The conspiracy formed quickly, for these wanted no new energy anyway. But the others! The ones from whom and for whom the gospel is written were aware of the staggering newness:

And they were all amazed, so that they questioned among themselves, saying, "What is this? A new teaching!" (Mark 1:27)

And they were filled with awe, and said to one another, "Who then is this, that even wind and sea obey him?" (Mark 4:41)

And many who heard him were astonished, saying, "Where did this man get all this? What is the wisdom given to him? What mighty works are wrought by his hands!" (Mark 6:2)

Mostly they were amazed, for more was going on than they could understand or account for, and so they marveled:

And amazement seized them all, and they glorified God and were filled with awe, saying, "We have seen strange things today." (Luke 5:26)

And all were astonished at the majesty of God. (Luke 9:43)

When the disciples heard this, they fell on their faces, and were filled with awe. (Matt 17:6)

But marveling at his answer they were silent. (Luke 22:26)

And they were astonished:

And when Jesus finished these sayings, the crowds were astonished at his teaching, for he taught them as one who had authority, and not as their scribes. (Matt 7:28)

And when the crowd heard it, they were astonished at his teaching. (Matt 22:33)

And he got into the boat with them and the wind ceased. And they were utterly astounded. (Mark 6:51)

And they were astonished beyond measure, saying, "He has done all things well; he even makes the deaf hear and the dumb speak." (Mark 7:37)

It is such a curious summary. We are accustomed to his work among the blind and lame and deaf, even though it scarcely fits our presumed world. Mostly, we do not live in a world where blind see again, where lame walk freely, or where deaf hear. We do not live there, and the stories of Jesus are so old and familiar that the wonder is blunted. Along with those conventional matters (conventional for Jesus, that is), however, appears leprosy. It is in healing leprosy that Jesus contradicts the norms of society concerning clean and unclean.[4] And in causing that rethinking of clean and unclean, Jesus was in fact calling into question all the moral distinctions upon which society was based.

With the moral distinctions called into question, all the sanctions for justifying the political and economic inequities are gone. The list is more staggering, for with these "conventional" healings comes the unthinkable and ultimate energizing of human persons out of death. Neither Luke nor the early church nor any of us understand what this means. It will not do to reason or argue or explain or calculate, for we are in the realm of the lyrical. We are called to doxology, for only doxology can adequately speak about the newness that came in Jesus. That strangeness of life from death should have been the last word, but the summary is kept securely in daily reality, for the last act is economic rehabilitation.[5] The poor have their debts canceled and their property restored. The last Messianic act is the end of royal confiscation. That supreme and most dangerous political act is more radical than life from death. On every imaginable front, Jesus is restoring the victims of the royal consciousness. If the managers of cleanness and uncleanness, the overseers of debt laws, and the officers of death have their verdicts overridden, they are obviously no longer in power. Surely this doxology contains a criticism, and that is evident in Luke 7:23. The actions of Jesus are a scandal, for they violate propriety, reason, and good public order.

But the narrative moves as quickly as possible from criticism to energy. The narrative does not want to linger with those who cannot face the news, and it does not grieve long for what is old and over. It looks to the future. It is a future given precisely where none was thinkable, an energizing that is in the tradition of Moses and Second Isaiah, though surely more radical in its historical concreteness:

> They feared him because all the multitude was astonished at his teaching. (Mark 11:18)
> The Pharisee was astonished to see that he did not first wash before dinner. (Luke 11:38)

Those words cover a variety of responses, which for our purposes do not need to be distinguished. They range from awe to surprise to terror to indignation. In general, Jesus' healings evoke amazement of a celebrative kind because they give life where all seemed hopeless. At the same time, his teaching evokes astonishment that includes a tone of negativity, resistance, and indignation, for Jesus contends with the conventions of his contemporaries. On the one hand, there is surprise that futures can be given to people who seemed to have no future. On the other hand, there is resentment that he would say and do as he did. In either case, his ministry evoked a passion and an energy that had disappeared in the old helplessness. Both his adherents and his enemies sensed the same thing: An unmanaged newness was coming, and it created a future quite different from the one that royal domination intended to permit.

Jesus' Teachings

The teachings of Jesus, of course, cannot be separated from the actions of his ministry. His teachings evoked radical energy, for they announced as sure and certain what had been denied by careful conspiracy. If anything, his teachings were more radical than his actions, for his teachings played out the implications of the harsh challenge and radical transformation at which his actions hinted. It was one thing to eat with outcasts, but it was far more radical to announce that the distinctions between insiders and outsiders were null and void. It was one thing to heal/forgive but quite another to announce that the conditions which had made one sick/guilty were now irrelevant. Of course the teachings cannot be separated from the actions, for it is the actions that give concreteness and reality to the teachings. The teachings, like the actions, are shattering, opening, and inviting. They conjure futures that had been closed off, and they indicate possibilities that had been defined as impossibilities. For our consideration it will be adequate to focus on the Beatitudes because they form an appropriate counterpart to the woes, especially as Luke has presented them (Luke 6:20-26).[6] For our purposes, the juxtaposition of woes and blessings is appropriate. The woes constitute the most radical criticism, for they are announcements and anticipations of death. The woes of Luke are pronounced against the rich (v. 24), the full (v. 25a), the ones who laugh (v. 25b), and the ones who enjoy social approval (v. 26)—which is to say that the death sentence is upon those who live fully and comfortably in this age without awareness or openness to the new future coming. In sharp contrast, the blessings are speeches of new energy, for they promise future well-being to those who are without hope. In the deathly world of riches, fullness, and uncritical laughter, those who now live in poverty, hunger, and grief are hopeless. They are indeed nonpersons consigned to nonhistory. They have no public existence, and so the public well-being can never extend to them. But the blessings open a new possibility. So the speech of Jesus, like the speech of the entire prophetic tradition, moves from woe to blessing, from judgment to hope, from criticism to energy. The alternative community to be shaped from the poor, hungry, and grieving is called to disengage from the woe pattern of life to end its fascination with that other ordering, and to embrace the blessing pattern.

The hope Jesus announces here is heavy and hard. It contrasts sharply with the cheap and cross-free hope of the royal consciousness. Hope is easy and flimsy for those who already have richness, fullness, and laughter now; but hope is hard for those who are denied the riches, prevented from fullness, and have no reason to laugh. The strangeness of this prophetic energizing is that it is addressed precisely to the nonpersons consigned to nonhistory. What is offered here is not a general moral reflection but a concrete offer to a specific constituency with a direct sanctioning of an alternative way. So the Lucan teaching is with "his eyes on his disciples" (Luke 6:20). His disciples constitute precisely the ones disengaged from the old ordering that is under criticism and lacks energy. His disciples are those who have been denied riches, prevented from fullness, and have no reason to laugh, those who are able to disengage from the woe pattern of life that can only lead to death, who have ended their fascination with that other ordering, and who can believe that these new words open up futures that the royal consciousness cannot offer.

These three blessing statements, surely a Lucan sample expressed as a longer list in Matthew, clearly express the issues of criticism and energy. Criticism to death is for those who have riches, for riches reflect the world of Pharaoh and Solomon and always concern the use of the goods of the brothers and sisters. The way of exploitation and confiscation leads to death. This is an old prophetic critique, but it is matched by this remarkable futuring. The new futuring of God is for those who have not only resisted these exploitative practices but have been victimized by them. The future will be given not to people in their fullness but to those who have been forcibly denied enough. The future is given to those who are experienced in groaning. The future is denied to those who have been cynical and calloused and self-deceiving enough to rejoice in the present ordering and are unable to grieve about the ruin toward which the royal community is headed.

Jesus' teaching in these hard sayings reflects two central issues of the prophetic tradition. First, the word is addressed to and received by a minority community consisting of marginal people. The prophetic word of criticism is addressed to the dominant community, but it will not be heard (Isa 6:9-10). The prophetic word of energy is addressed never to the dominant community but only to those who are denied the pseudo-energy and power of the royal consciousness. Second, the promissory, prophetic word concerns a radical turn, a break with the old rationality, and a discontinuity between what has been and what will be. Thus the teaching presumed a contrast between that to which we cling and a future for which we yearn. The ministry of Jesus, like the ministry of Second Isaiah, happens in the space between the clinging and the yearning. If there is only clinging, then the words are only critical. If there is yearning, there is a chance that the words are energizing. The staggering works of Jesus—feeding, healing, casting out, forgiving—happened not to those who held on to the old order but to those who yearned because the old order had failed them or squeezed them out.

The Beatitudes are cunningly articulated to sharpen the contrasts. The woes describe the royal consciousness and, in that situation, there is mostly the energy of fear. By contrast, those who have now broken with that consciousness, whose lives are organized against those values, and who know that the royal community cannot keep it promises, are the ones who are opened to another future. That future is an unqualified yes from God. The energy of this blessing word comes in the reality that God has alternative futures, that he is free to bestow them, and that futures are not derived from or determined by the present. Thus this teaching is faithful to the work of Moses, who created an underived community. It reflects the joy of Second Isaiah, who evoked a community not derived from the Babylonian reality. And, like Second Isaiah, Jesus is able to articulate a future that is distinctly different from an unbearable present. But that future is energizing only for those for whom the present has become unbearable. For those people and that community the abrasion takes the form of promise; the judgment takes the form of energy;

the condemnation takes the form of hope. Believers in that future given by God are able to sing and to dance, to heal and to forgive. All those actions that the numb cannot take are given to believers in that future.

The people who receive the compassion of Jesus experience it as authority. They had been living unauthorized lives because they knew that the claimant kings were both unauthorized themselves and incapable of authorizing anyone else. But the vulnerable solidarity of Jesus with the poor, empty, and grieving was found to have an authenticity and a power unlike what they had known. They found him to be radically disinterested and therefore profoundly *for us*. That is exactly the learning Moses' Israel was given about Yahweh. Unlike the pharaohs and the gods of the pharaohs, Yahweh was disinterested, and so his intervention had power and authority. The authority of Jesus, his power to transform strangely, was found precisely in his own poverty, hunger, and grieving over the death of his people. In his poverty he had the power to make many rich (2 Cor 8:9). In his hunger he had the capacity to fill others. In his capacity to grieve he had the power to bring joy and wholeness to others. In his person, which was nonperson in the eyes of the pseudokings, he had the authority to give futures to his constituency.

Jesus' Resurrection

Such a way of discerning the sovereign power of his gracious compassion leads directly to the resurrection of Jesus. The resurrection of Jesus is the ultimate energizing for the new future. The wrenching of Friday had left only the despair of Saturday (Luke 24:21), and the disciples had no reason to expect Sunday after that Friday. The resurrection cannot be explained on the basis of the previously existing reality. The resurrection can only be received and affirmed and celebrated as the new action of God, whose province it is to create new futures for people and to let them be amazed in the midst of despair.

So it is my concern to show that the resurrection is faithful to and can only be understood in terms of the characteristically surprising energizing of the promises of the prophets. The resurrection of Jesus is not to be understood in good liberal fashion as a spiritual development in the church. Nor should it be too quickly handled as an oddity in the history of God or an isolated act of God's power. Rather, it is the ultimate act of prophetic energizing in which a new history is initiated. It is a new history open to all but peculiarly received by the marginal victims of the old order. The fully energized Lord of the church is not some godly figure in the sky but the slain Lamb who stood outside the royal domain and was punished for it.

Without detracting from the historical singularity of the resurrection, we can also affirm that it is of a piece with the earlier appearances of an alternative future by the prophetic word. The resurrection of Jesus made possible a future for the disinherited. In the same way, the alternative community of Moses was given a new future by the God who brought freedom for slaves by his powerful word, which both dismantled and created a future and which engaged in radical energizing and radical criticizing. In the same way, the resurrection of Jesus made possible a future for the disinherited, as did the newness announced by Second Isaiah. The nonpeople in the nonhistory of Babylon were given a homecoming like the poor, hungry, and grieving in the history of Jesus.

The resurrection is a genuinely historical event in which the dead one rules. But that genuinely historical event has important political dimensions, as is recognized especially in Matthew. On the one hand, it is seen as a threat to the regime (Matt 28:11-15), whereas, on the other hand, the risen Jesus announces his new royal authority. He is now the king who displaces the king. His resurrection is the end of the nonhistory taught in the royal school and a new history begins for those who stood outside of history. This new history gives persons new identities (Matt 28:19) and a new ethic (28:20), even as it begins on the seashore among the dead enslavers (Exod 14:30).

7

A Note on the Practice of Ministry

Summary

First let me summarize the argument. Something new happened in history with the Exodus and the Moses movement. On the one hand, Moses intended the dismantling of the oppressive empire of Pharaoh; and on the other hand, he intended the formation of a new community focused on the religion of God's freedom and the politics of justice and compassion. The *dismantling* begins in the groans and complaints of his people; the *energizing* begins in the doxologies of the new community.

The Moses movement is too radical for Israel, however; therefore, soon there is an attempt to counter the new history of energy. The old history of Pharaoh is continued in the monarchy of Israel. The monarchy, with its interest in self-securing, is effective in *silencing the criticism and denying the energizing;* but the kings never seem able to silence the prophets for long. The prophets of Israel continue the radical movement of Moses in the face of royal reality. On the one hand, *Jeremiah practices the radical criticism* against the royal consciousness. He does this essentially by conjuring a funeral and bringing the grief of dying Israel to public expression. He does this to penetrate the numb denial of the royal community, which pretended that things must go on forever. On the other hand, *Second Isaiah practices radical energizing* against the royal consciousness. He does this by conjuring an enthronement and bringing the amazement of rebirthed Israel to public expression. He does this to penetrate the weary despair of the royal community, which assumed things were over forever.

Jesus of Nazareth, a prophet, and more than a prophet, I argue, practiced in most radical form the main elements of prophetic ministry and imagination. On the one hand, he practiced criticism of the deathly world around him. The dismantling was fully wrought in his crucifixion, in which he himself embodied the thing dismantled. On the other hand, he practiced the energizing of the new future given by God. This energizing was fully manifested in his resurrection, in which he embodied the new future given by God.

Ministry

This note is concerned with the practice of ministry. Without this note the entire discussion lacks the concreteness appropriate to discussions of the prophetic. Without precluding peculiar ministries in special places, it is presumed that the practice of ministry is done by those who stand in conventional places of parish life and other forms of ministry derived from that model. We cling to the conviction that prophetic ministry can and must be practiced there, although many things militate against it. The ministry is, first of all, consumed by the daily round of busyness that cannot be ignored; perhaps that daily pressure may be reduced, but it cannot be ignored. In addition, the ministry most often exists in congregations that are bourgeois, if not downright obdurate, and in which there is no special openness to or support of prophetic ministry.

Other things can be said as well, and I have tried to say some of them in this book. I have tried to say that prophetic ministry does not consist of spectacular acts of social crusading or of abrasive measures of indignation. Rather, prophetic ministry consists of offering an alternative perception of reality and in letting people see their own history in the light of God's freedom and his will for justice. The issues of God's freedom and his will for justice are not always and need not be expressed primarily in the big issues of the day. They can be discerned wherever people try to live together and show concern for their shared future and identity. So these dimensions of prophetic ministry arise from our study:

1. The task of prophetic ministry is to evoke an alternative community that knows it is about different things in different ways. And that alternative community has a variety of relationships with the dominant community.

2. The practice of prophetic ministry is not some special thing done two days a week. Rather, it is done in, with, and under all the acts of ministry—as much in counseling as in preaching, as much in liturgy as in education. It concerns a stance and posture or a hermeneutic about the world of death and the word of life that can be brought to light in every context.

3. Prophetic ministry seeks to penetrate the numbness in order to face the body of death in which we are caught. Clearly, the numbness sometimes evokes from us rage and anger, but the numbness is more likely to be penetrated by grief and lament. Death, and that is our state, does not require indignation as much as it requires anguish and the sharing in the pain. The public sharing of pain is one way to let the reality sink in and let the death go.

4. Prophetic ministry seeks to penetrate despair so that new futures can be believed in and embraced by us. There is a yearning for energy in a world grown weary: "The age has lost its youth, and the times begin to grow old" (2 Esd 14:10). And we do know that the only act that energizes is a word, a gesture, an act that believes in our future and affirms it to us disinterestedly.

In a society that knows about initiative and self-actualization and countless other things, the capacity to lament the death of the old world is nearly lost. In a society strong on self-congratulation, the capacity to receive in doxology the new world being given is nearly lost. Grief and praise are ways of prophetic criticism and energy, which can be more intentional even in our age.

Radical Faith as Gift

As I reflect on ministry, and especially my ministry, I know in the hidden places that the real restraints are not in my understanding or in the receptivity of other people. Rather, the restraints come from my own unsureness about this perception. I discover that I am as bourgeois and obdurate as any to whom I might minister. I, like most of the others, am unsure that the royal road is not the best and the royal community the one which governs the real "goodies." I, like most of the others, am unsure that the alternative community inclusive of the poor, hungry, and grieving is really the wave of God's future. We are indeed "like people, like priest" (Hos 4:9). That very likely is the situation among many of us in ministry, and there is no unanguished way out of it. It does make clear to us that our ministry will always be practiced through our own conflicted selves. No prophet has ever borne an unconflicted message, even until Jesus (compare Mark 14:36). Thus the Beatitudes end in realism (Luke 6:22-23). Also, it reminds us again that such radical faith is not an achievement; for if it were, we would will it and be done. Rather, it is a gift, and we are left to wait receptively, to watch and to pray.

Perhaps our own situation credits what we have suggested here. We ourselves shall likely move in and out, precisely because of our poor capacity to grieve the death in our own lives and to be amazed at the new futures. We are not more skilled in that than all the other children of the royal community, and therefore we must engage in the same painful practices of becoming who we are called to be. I have come to think that there is no more succinct summary of prophetic ministry than the statement of Jesus: "Blessed are you that weep now, for you shall laugh" (Luke 6:21), or, more familiarly, "Blessed are those who mourn, for they shall be comforted" (Matt 5:4).

Jesus' concern was, finally, for the joy of the kingdom. That is what he promised, and to that he invited people. But he was clear that rejoicing in that future required a grieving about the present order.[1] Jesus takes a quite dialectical two-age view of things. He will not be like one-world liberals who view the present world as the only one, nor will he be like the unworldly who yearn for the future with an unconcern about the present. There is work to be done in the present. There is grief work to be done in the present that the future may come. There is mourning to be done for those who do not know of the deathliness of their situation. There is mourning to be done with those who know pain and suffering and lack the power or freedom to bring it to speech. The saying is a harsh one, for it sets this grief work as the precondition of joy. It announces that those who have not cared enough to grieve will not know joy.

The mourning is a precondition in another way too. It is not a formal, external requirement but rather the only door and route to joy. Seen in that context, Jesus' saying about weeping and laughing is not just a neat aphorism but a summary of the entire theology of the cross. Only that kind of anguished disengagement permits fruitful yearning, and only the public embrace of deathliness permits newness to come. We are at the edge of knowing this in our personal lives, for we understand a bit of the processes of grieving.[2] But we have yet to learn and apply it to the reality of society. And finally, we have yet to learn it about God, who grieves in ways hidden from us and who waits to rejoice until his promises are fully kept.

A Postscript on Practice

In the end, of course, "prophetic imagination" is not simply "a good idea." It is a concrete practice that is undertaken by real believers who share the conviction of grief and hope that escapes the restraints of dominant culture. It is my hope that my exposition of prophetic imagination is intimately connected to concrete practice and that it may, on occasion, evoke, generate, and authorize such concrete practice.

Thus at the end of my exposition I take the liberty of identifying some concrete practices of prophetic imagination that are under way in concrete subcommunities of grief and hope that engage in resistance and alternative. Of course I do not suggest at all that this list is generated by my exposition, but only that the examples I cite are typical and representative of what is possible for the church in its enactment of prophetic imagination. Obviously the list I present is in large part happenstance and subjective and concerns the practices known to me. The reader surely knows other such typical practices and is invited to add to the list. The ones I think of include the following.

In Atlanta, close to my own experience:
Plymouth Harbor. This is a day-care facility housed by my local UCC Church, Central Congregational Church. Led by the relentless and persistent Pam Rapp, it cares on a daily basis for

persons suffering from dementia, Alzheimer's disease, and other forms of senior dysfunction. The care is necessarily person-to-person, labor intensive, and extraordinarily demanding of both staff and a host of volunteers.

Family Counseling Services Urban Ministries. A network of urban ministries presided over by cunning and knowing Bob Lupton that aims at rehabilitation and restoration of communities that are economically disadvantaged and consequently crime threatened. FCS operates entrepreneurially and taps effectively into the resources of corporate capitalism in the enactment of its dreams.

Open Door. A food-and-shelter community of worship and care with Presbyterian connections. This agency, led by the shrill Ed Loring and the determined Murphy Davis, in addition to self-styled "band aids," maintains a shrill and steady voice of dissent so that the poor remain visible in the city.

Beyond Atlanta, the following have come to my attention:

Jimmy Carter, in his stunning post-presidential vocation, works on a large international scale at political reconciliation, all the while keeping his hand concretely in on-site hammer-and-nails work with Habitat for Humanity.

The Industrial Areas Foundation (IAF) is a community organizing effort derived from the passion and strategies of Saul Alinsky. My contact has been with Ernesto Cortez, officed in Austin, Texas, a regional office for the Southwest. This remarkable effort at mobilizing communities for the sake of shared well-being includes passionate staff people, spirited volunteers, and institutional, congregational support that takes on large urban issues concerned with social justice in the face of fearful privatization.

Watts Street Baptist Church (Durham, North Carolina), where T. Melvin Williams Jr. is the pastor, characteristically begins its worship services not with conventional praise but with lament Psalms, with the "public processing of pain." That congregation, moreover, is part of a Durham church coalition that "regularly holds prayer vigils at the site of each violent death" in Durham. The ritual marks the accession and the loss liturgically and thereby creates a place for protest and grief in response to the violence that destroys life.

Church Health Center, sponsored by a church coalition of hundreds of congregations in Memphis, has established an extensive, first-rate health care system for the poor in that city where poverty savages too many. Alongside deep and crucial church support and participation, the center mobilizes the active support of hundreds of dentists and doctors plus the resources of a large hospital that has made building space available. The moving force for this immense project is Scott Morris. Morris combines medical expertise and theological sensitivity, a capacity for organizational effectiveness and abundant people skills. Around his passion and vision have gathered a large prophetic populace that is resolved to connect the healing capacity of God to the poor who are deprived of normal health care delivery.

Finally, in this quite personal and subjective list to which many other items, names, and efforts should be added, I want to report a most fortuitous happening. On the very day that I was writing this paragraph (September 26, 2000), it happened that Andrew McAuley Smith, pastor of Westminster Presbyterian Church in Charlotte, shared with me a copy of his 1999 D.Min. thesis from Princeton Seminary. He was generous to give me a copy that of course caught my attention because it is titled, *Prophets in the Pews: Testing Walter Brueggemann's Thesis in The Prophetic Imagination in the Practice of Ministry.*[1] Smith has taken my book and has understood that the test of its exposition is actual, concrete practice of the faithful in the life of the world, which for his particular study focuses upon the social crisis evoked by racism. After an alert summary of my argument, Smith organizes his response in two ways.

First, he offers a working definition of white racism and considers the perception of racism as offered by three towering prophetic figures:

1. Bartolome de Las Casas (1474–1566), a Spaniard who came to the "new world" along with the first colonialists after Christopher Columbus, in the midst of the Spanish genocide against the native population of Haiti and Cuba. He came on an evangelizing mission of the church but became single-handedly a vigorous, noticeable force in defense of the "Indians" against European rapaciousness.

2. Dietrich Bonhoeffer (1906–1945), a better-known German theologian who took his bold stand early against the "Aryan clause" of German National Socialism, and almost single-handedly summoned the Confessing Church in German to see what was at stake in the racism of National Socialism against Jews—for which he risked and eventually sacrificed his life.

3. Martin Luther King Jr. (1929–1969), best known among us as a prophet for racial justice whose life was given over to—and taken by—that cause.[2]

Second, on the basis of that data, Smith articulates his research project, which is to examine the outreach ministry of Westminster Presbyterian Church in Charlotte as it concerns racial issues. He examines twin hypotheses that are to be tested through his research:

1. Lay outreach ministries that cross racial and socioeconomic barriers in Charlotte, North Carolina, are serving as prophetic voices in confronting white racism in the Southern church.

2. Lay outreach ministries that cross racial and socioeconomic barriers in Charlotte, North Carolina, are simply enabling the volunteers to "feel good" about participating in acts of charity, and therefore are not addressing the deeper issues related to white racism in the Southern church.[3]

Smith's conclusion confirms his first hypothesis. His further reflection on the prophetic dimension of ministry is this:

The prophetic witness of the church is not to be identified in some *specific functions* of ministry and not in others. Prophetic witness is a mind-set. It is a countercultural consciousness of how the community of faith sees all things. Therefore, to ask the question if one specific group of ministries are "prophetic voices" might imply that other ministries within the same church setting are not. The mere presence of a question considering the prophetic nature of a specific group of ministries within a local congregation is in danger of misunderstanding the nature of prophetic witness. This project served to remind me that *all* functions of the church can and should be prophetic voices that serve to criticize the dominant culture around us while energizing the faithful. Pastoral care can be a prophetic ministry. Preaching can be prophetic ministry. Sunday school classes can be prophetic ministry (even session meetings can be prophetic ministry!).

Thus, the essential question for the church is whether or not its prophetic voice has been co-opted into the culture of the day. The community of God's people who are striving to remain faithful to the whole counsel of God's Word *will* be prophetic voices crying out in the wilderness of the dominant culture of our day.[4]

Aside from the particular enquiry that concerns Smith, his study is a rich and suggestive way in which the themes exposited in my book may engage with actual ecclesial practice.

While the environment of technological consumerism in the United States is not a welcoming habitat for prophetic ministry, these several instances of prophetic ministry that I have cited are grounds for taking heart. Obviously every reader can add to that list of local efforts at resistance and alternatives. The interplay between *prophetic texts heard imaginatively* and *concrete practice* is a defining one for the church that will become more crucial and more difficult, and perhaps more joyous, in time to come.

In Retrospect (PI at Forty)

Forty years is a long time for a book! I am gratified—the reader will understand—that many readers continue to judge that the book has contemporary interpretive currency.

As I look back on the forty years since I first wrote *The Prophetic Imagination*, the one particular change that I might make in my articulation of a prophetic paradigm is this: I used the phrase "royal consciousness" to refer to the socio-ideological context in which Israel's ancient prophets performed. I would now alter "royal consciousness" to "totalism," thus making the reference more readily transferable to other contexts like that of our own in late capitalism. I have learned the term "totalism" from Robert Lifton, who, in his study of variety of ideological regimes, has identified the characteristic, recurring practices of such regimes that serve to "totalize" the claim of regime.[1] Behind Lifton, one might also refer to the "totality" of Emmanuel Levinas.[2] The term "totalism" refers to a socio-ideological arrangement in which hegemonic ideology takes up all the social space and allows for no alternative possibility. Its claim is "total"!

It is fashionable among many so-called "religious progressives" to refer to any advocacy for social justice as "prophetic." There is nothing objectionable about such usage. It is worth noting, however, that "prophetic" in ancient Israel does not refer precisely to matters of social justice. The prophetic in ancient Israel rather is a

"God-performance" in which YHWH, the Lord of the covenant, is voiced as a real character and lively agent (a claim that is surely an embarrassment to many religious progressives), funded by old narratives, songs, and poems. It is because prophetic utterance is a "God-performance" that the prophetic oracles are regularly marked by "Thus saith the Lord," or "The word of the Lord came to me." That is, in these utterances and actions, the prophetic hosts a world in which the agency, will, and purpose of God are effective and to be taken with utmost seriousness. This, moreover, amid a regime that determinedly dismissed such claims and relied instead on a tepid god who functioned simply as patron of the regime.

Such prophetic insistence asserts that YHWH has a specific will and purpose (known in the Torah) that lies outside the totalism of the day and that will not be mocked or countermanded by the practice of that totalism. When social or cultic practices violate or contradict that purpose, God works judgment, so say the prophets, through various agents and mediations—sometimes "natural" crises, sometimes through other nations. That divine purpose does, of course, concern socioeconomic justice for the vulnerable (widows, orphans, immigrants), but it also sometimes concerns the disciplines of holiness that fail to match the singularity of God's people to the singularity of God (see Lev 19:2; Ezek 22:26). When the "prophetic" among us concerns social justice without the claim of divine agency, it is possible, as with many religious progressives, to contain social justice within the purview of the totalism—that is, without elemental transformation. It is the recurring claim of Israel's prophets, however, that the claim will not and is not contained within the totalism of any regime, not even that of the holy city of Jerusalem.

Such prophetic insistence affirms the freedom of God to act outside of, beyond, and in contradiction to the totalism. It can, for that reason, anticipate the divine work of newness that is voiced as divine promise. Thus, the prophets can confidently assert, "The days are surely coming," or "in that day." The anticipated day of God's newness is an authentic newness. It is not derived from or extrapolated from present life circumstance. Thus in both acts of *prophetic judgment* and *prophetic promise*, the prophets speak a world of divine resolve that owes nothing to the present totalism. The totalism does not believe it can or will be terminated; it does not, moreover, believe any new alternative is possible. It is the character of God, known here in poetic articulation as sovereign who will not be mocked by the pretensions of the totalism and as promise-keeper who will not be contained in or foiled by the dead-ends of the totalism that is the subject of the prophets.

The reason prophetic utterance evokes the lethal hostility of the totalism, I judge, is not simply because of an advocacy for social justice, though the prophets did indeed advocate systemic justice. The reason for hostility, rather, is because the enunciation of the God of the covenant (who is the creator God) renders the claims of the totalism penultimate, while every totalizing regime (as in "Make America Great Again") presents itself as ultimate. Prophetic deconstruction dismisses the ultimacy of allegiance and submission expected by the totalism. The enunciation of this God undermines all such pretensions.

In both judgment and hope, prophetic articulation—in elusive poetic form—voices the *interruption* of the known controlled world of the totalism and the *emergence* of an alternative world that is dramatically other than the world managed by the totalism. The prophets voice a world other than the visible, palpable world that is in front of their hearers. For that reason, prophetic utterance must perforce be "imaginative," an act of imagination by word and image that evokes and hosts a world other than the one readily available. Thus the prophets, with their passionate rootage in tradition, their passionate grasp of social reality, and their passionate force of language, imagine the present world under threat and judgment, even while the regime continues to imagine itself as absolute and abiding. The prophets can even imagine the termination of the Holy City over which the regime presides. Thus the prophets, conversely, imagine a new world coming outside the totalism that the totalism thinks is impossible. They imagine a new sociopolitical, this-world emergence beyond the capacity of the regime. The totalism imagines itself absolute to perpetuity, while the prophetic imagination—in contradiction—imagines an old world ending and a new world emerging. It is a *contest of imaginations* that admits no easy resolution but that puts the hearer in crisis between a *failed imagination* and a *new inexplicable imagination*.[3] In the formation of Scripture's canon, that contest between imaginations is resolved on behalf of prophetic imagination while dismissing the imagination of the totalism. Prophetic imagination is judged in the canon to be adequately truthful, even when on occasion historical events say otherwise.

It has become clear to me, albeit belatedly, that the paradigm I have offered in this book has functioned as leitmotif for much of my subsequent work. Thus, I have further explicitly exposited such thought in *Hopeful Imagination*, in *Reality, Grief, and Hope*, and most recently in *The Practice of Prophetic Imagination*, as well as less explicitly in many of my publications.[4] While my journal articles have been scattered and varied, I think that two of my most durable journal articles further serve the same paradigm. First, in "The Costly Loss of Lament," I have considered what could happen—as does happen in the bourgeoisie church and in bourgeoisie political culture—when the ancient practices of lament, protest, and complaint are silenced and avoided in the interest of happy, uncritical well-being.[5] In civic culture, the loss of lament invites denial and so enhances the dominant social system as though it were beyond failure or critique. In the church, with such a loss, the gospel becomes one of unmitigated happiness where "never is heard a discouraging word." Many pastors, moreover, are paid to sustain exactly such a practice. But of course, in prophetic realism (as with real-life realism), such an illusion is unsustainable because there is much about which to lament, protest, and complain. The "costly loss" is to sign on for the illusion of well-being, or in theology it is an exercise in a "Theology of Glory" to the disregard of a summoning "Theology of the Cross."[6]

Second, in my article, "The Liturgy of Abundance and the Myth of Scarcity," it becomes clear that "scarcity" is an element in a strategy for injustice.[7] A regime that operates with a claim of scarcity can legitimate hoarding, accumulation, and eventually monopoly to the disregard of the needs of others, even when such strategies evoke and legitimate the violence of the strong against the weak. (Thus, we have "class war" that is characteristically conducted from above; as Warren Buffett has observed in our economy: "There is a class war and we are winning.") Israel's doxologies of abundance (as in Psalms 104 and 145) affirm the generative generosity of the creator God. Thus, the sloganeering of scarcity contradicts the claims of the generativity of the creator. And of course, the endless frantic acquisitiveness evoked by market ideology (our specific form of totalism) serves to counter the claims of faith in a way that has real-life practical consequences.[8]

I need hardly attest that the profound tension between *totalism* and *prophetic imagination* is ferociously active among us as Donald Trump has eagerly become the point person for such a totalism. His mantra "Make America Great Again" is a heavy-handed ideology with a validation of racist accents and an uncritical embrace of the exceptionalism of "the American Dream." President Trump, however, did not create this ideology, which is very old in the lore of Euro-American exceptionalism, operative already in the early Puritanism of Cotton Mather. The outcome of that unapologetic ideology is *the monetizing of all social relationships, the commoditization of all social possibilities*, and *the endless production of dispensable persons* who have no legitimate membership in the totalism. One may quibble about detail, but the main thrust of market ideology among us is beyond dispute.

For that reason, it follows that ours is a time for prophetic imagination, the capacity to host a world other than the one sponsored and legitimated by market ideology. In the contemporary practice of prophetic imagination, it will be important

* to move the church from its comfortable habit of charity to issues of justice;

* to move the church to a systemic awareness of ways to "follow the money";
* to show the ways in which the old traditions of the God of the covenant makes righteousness, justice, and faithfulness central to common life in a way that resituates-money, power, and wisdom (see Jer 9:23–24; Matt 23:23); and
* to see how a theology of the cross contradicts our more comfortable, convenient theologies of glory.

It is a time for the courage and freedom to engage in contestation with the totalism among us that is killing in its force and authority.

I am grateful to Fortress Press and its editors for continuing to make this book available, and for marking it on this anniversary occasion. I am grateful to a host of readers (including pastors, nuns, teachers, and students) who have found the book to be a resource for serious interdisciplinary engagement. Now as always, prophetic imagination depends upon great intentionality, and it requires a host of reliable companions on the way from a failed world under judgment to a new world of good-news possibility. That "way" is one of *relinquishing* what has failed (which we are likely to treasure) and *receiving* what God will give. It is a move from *scarcity to abundance* that is likely routed *through lament to doxology.*

Walter Brueggemann
Advent, 2017

Abbreviations

AAR	American Academy of Religion
AB	Anchor Bible
ABD	*Anchor Bible Dictionary*
ATR	*Anglican Theological Review*
BA	*Biblical Archaeologist*
B.C.E.	Before the Common Era
BTB	*Biblical Theology Bulletin*
CBQ	*Catholic Biblical Quarterly*
ChrCent	*Christian Century*
EcRev	*The Ecumenical Review*
FOTL	The Forms of the Old Testament Literature
GBS	Guides to Biblical Scholarship
HBT	*Horizons in Biblical Theology*
IDBS	*Interpreter's Dictionary of the Bible, Supplementary Volume*
Interp	*Interpretation*
ITC	International Theological Commentary
JAAR	*Journal of the American Academy of Religion*
JBL	*Journal of Biblical Literature*
JSOT	*Journal for the Study of the Old Testament*
JSOTSup	JSOT Supplement Series
KAT	Kommentar zum Alten Testament
OBT	Overtures to Biblical Theology

OTL	Old Testament Library
PTMS	Pittsburgh Theological Monograph Series
SAA	State Archives of Assyria
SAAS	State Archives of Assyria Studies
SBL	Society of Biblical Literature
SBT	Studies in Biblical Theology
SBTS	Sources for Biblical and Theological Study
SWBA	The Social World of Biblical Antiquity Series
ThTo	*Theology Today*
TUMSR	Trinity University Monograph Series in Religion
VT	*Vetus Testamentum*
VTS	VT Supplements
WW	*Word and World*
ZAW	*Zeitschrift für die alttestamentliche Wissenschaft*
ZTK	*Zeitschrift für Theologie und Kirche*

Notes

Foreword

1. For example, on the role of imagination in interpretation, see Walter Brueggemann, *Texts Under Negotiation: The Bible and Postmodern Imagination* (Minneapolis: Fortress Press, 1993); on imagination in the texts, see Walter Brueggemann, *David's Truth in Israel's Imagination and Memory*, 2nd ed. (Minneapolis: Fortress Press, 2002).

2. Kathleen M. O'Connor, *Jeremiah: Pain and Promise* (Minneapolis: Fortress Press, 2011).

3. See Thomas Piketty, *Capital in the Twenty-First Century*, trans. Arthur Goldhammer (Cambridge, MA: Belknap Press of Harvard University Press, 2014).

4. See, for example, Lawrence Mishel, Elise Gould, and Josh Bivens, "Wage Stagnation in Nine Charts," Economic Policy Institute, January 6, 2015, https://tinyurl.com/ybnuk95l.

5. See Rana Foroohar, *Makers and Takers: How Wall Street Destroyed Main Street* (New York: Crown Business, 2016).

6. Martin Luther King Jr., "I Have a Dream," in *The Autobiography of Martin Luther King, Jr.*, ed. Clayborne Carson (New York: Warner Books, 1998), 224.

Preface to the Second Edition

1. Norman K. Gottwald, *The Tribes of Yahweh: A Sociology of the Religion of Liberated Israel, 1250–1050 B.C.* (Maryknoll, N.Y.: Orbis, 1979).

2. Robert R. Wilson, *Prophecy and Society in Ancient Israel* (Philadelphia: Fortress Press, 1980).

3. Phyllis Trible, *God and the Rhetoric of Sexuality,* OBT (Philadelphia: Fortress Press, 1978). Trible's more recent book, *Rhetorical Criticism: Context, Method, and the Book of Jonah,* GBS (Minneapolis: Fortress Press, 1994), presents the method in more programmatic fashion.

4. Paul Ricoeur has famously distinguished among "the world behind the text," "the world within the text," and "the world in front of the text."

5. Among the more important recent discussions of the issue is Garrett Green, *Theology, Hermeneutics, and Imagination: The Crisis of Interpretation at the End of Modernity* (Cambridge: Cambridge University Press, 2000). The key issue in imagination is the extent to which it is reflective of a given and the extent to which it is generative of a new given. Green is cautious on the matter but in his most recent book seems to move a bit in a more constructivist direction.

6. Frederick Asals, *Flannery O'Connor: The Imagination of Extremity* (Athens: University of Georgia Press, 1982).

7. Ibid., 198–233.

8. Ibid., 213.

9. Ibid., 215.

10. Ibid., 221, with a defining quote from Abraham Heschel, *The Prophets* (New York: Harper & Row, 1962), 10.

11. Ibid., 221.

12. Ibid., 226, quoting Heschel, 179.

13. Ibid., 226.

14. Ibid., 227.

15. Ibid., 228, with a quote from Heschel, 7.

16. Ibid., 233.

17. Wilson, *Prophecy and Society,* 69–83 and passim.

18. William T. Cavanaugh, *Torture and Eucharist: Theology, Politics, and the Body of Christ* (Oxford: Blackwell Publishers, 1998).

19. Lawrence Thornton, *Imagining Argentina* (New York: Doubleday, 1987).

20. Cavanaugh, *Torture and Eucharist,* 278, with a quote from Thornton, 131.

21. Lawrence, *Imagining Argentina,* 65, quoted by Cavanaugh, *Torture and Eucharist,* 279.

22. Cavanaugh, *Torture and Eucharist,* 279.

Chapter 1

1. To be sure, the prophet lives in tension with the tradition. While the prophet is indeed shaped by the tradition, breaking free from the tradition to assert the new freedom of God is also characteristic of the prophet. Compare Walther Zimmerli, "Prophetic Proclamation and Reinterpretation," in *Tradition and Theology in the Old Testament*, ed. Douglas A. Knight (Philadelphia: Fortress Press, 1977), 69–100. More broadly, Joseph Blenkinsopp, *Prophecy and Canon: A Contribution to the Study of Jewish Origins,* Studies of Judaism and Christianity in Antiquity 3 (Notre Dame, Ind.: Notre Dame Univ. Press, 1977), has explored the authority found in the ongoing tension between prophet and tradition.

2. Formally this argument is informed by the sociology of Peter Berger and Thomas Luckmann, *The Social Construction of Reality: A Treatise in the Sociology of Knowledge* (Garden City, N.Y.: Doubleday, 1966); Peter Berger, *The Sacred Canopy: Elements of a Sociological Theory of Religion* (Garden City, N.Y.: Doubleday, 1967); Thomas Luckmann, *The Invisible Religion: The Problem of Religion in Modern Society* (New York: Macmillan, 1967). But our concern is with the substance of prophetic ministry and not simply with formal understandings. In terms of substance, the issue has been well put by Douglas John Hall, *Lighten Our Darkness: Toward an Indigenous Theology of the Cross* (Philadelphia: Westminster, 1976).

3. The data on prophetic ecstasy has been summarized by Johannes Lindblom, *Prophecy in Ancient Israel* (Philadelphia: Fortress Press, 1973; original publication, 1962). Compare V. Epstein, "Was Saul Also Among the Prophets?" *ZAW* 81 (1969): 287–304; Robert R. Wilson, "Prophecy and Ecstasy: A Reexamination," *JBL* 98 (1979): 321–37, reprinted in *Community, Identity, and Ideology: Social Science Approaches to the Hebrew Bible,* ed. C. E. Carter and C. L. Meyers (Winona Lake, Ind.: Eisenbrauns, 1996), 404–22. Note should be made of Thomas Overholt's comparative work, *Channels of Prophecy: The Social Dynamics of Prophetic Activity* (Minneapolis: Fortress Press, 1989).

On Mari and comparative materials on institutional prophecy, see F. Ellenmeier, *Prophetie in Mari und Israel* (Herzberg: E. Jungfer, 1968); John H. Hayes, "Prophetism at Mari and Old Testament Parallels," *ATR* 49 (1967) 397–409; Herbert B. Huffmon, "Prophecy in the Mari Letters," *BA* 31 (1968) 101–24, and his summary articles: "Prophecy in the Ancient Near East," in *IDBS* (1976) 697–700, and "Prophecy (Ancient Near East)," in *ABD* (New York: Doubleday, 1992) 5:477–82; Abraham Malamat, "A Forerunner of Biblical Prophecy: The Mari Documents," in *Ancient Israelite Religion: Essays in Honor of Frank Moore Cross*, ed. P. D. Miller Jr. et al. (Philadelphia: Fortress Press, 1987), 33–52; idem, "Prophecy at Mari," in *The Place Is Too Small for Us: The Israelite Prophets in Recent Scholarship*, ed. R. P. Gordon, SBTS 5 (Winona Lake, Ind.: Eisenbrauns, 1995), 50–73.

On Neo-Assyrian prophecy, see Martti Nissinen, *References to Prophecy in Neo-Assyrian Sources,* SAAS 7 (Helsinki: Neo-Assyrian Text Corpus Project, 1998); Simo Parpola, *Assyrian Prophecies,* SAA 9 (Helsinki: Helsinki Univ. Press, 1997).

4. R. E. Clements, *Prophecy and Tradition: Growing Points in Theology* (Atlanta: John Knox, 1975); R. E. Clements, *Prophecy and Covenant,* SBT 1/43 (Naperville, Ill.: Allenson, 1965). This judgment, I am aware, is against the current tendency of scholarship. Thus, for example, Ronald Clements in his more recent *Prophecy and Tradition* has drawn back somewhat from his earlier position in *Covenant and Prophecy.* There is currently the reassertion of a kind of neo-Wellhausian perspective, and that may be an important corrective to the synthesis of Gerhard von Rad. Nonetheless, I would urge that we are on sound ground if we take as our beginning point Moses as the paradigmatic prophet who sought to evoke in Israel an alternative consciousness.

5. George E. Mendenhall, *The Tenth Generation: The Origins of the Biblical Tradition* (Baltimore: Johns Hopkins Univ. Press, 1973), chaps. 7–8; Norman K. Gottwald, "Domain Assumptions and Societal Models in the Study of Pre-Monarchic Israel," in *Congress Volume: Edinburgh 1974,* VTS 28 (Leiden: Brill, 1978), 89–100, reprinted in Gottwald, *The Hebrew Bible in Its Social World and in Ours*, Semeia Studies (Atlanta: Scholars, 1993), 5–15; idem, *The Tribes of Yahweh: A Sociology of the Religion of Liberated Israel, 1250–1050 B.C.E.* (Maryknoll, N.Y.: Orbis, 1979).

6. See the collection of essays in *The Bible and Liberation: Political and Social Hermeneutics*, ed. Norman K. Gottwald and Richard A. Horsley, rev. ed., Bible and Liberation Series (Maryknoll, N.Y.: Orbis, 1993).

7. This point has been most forcefully made by M. Douglas Meeks, *God the Economist: The Doctrine of God and Political Economy* (Minneapolis: Fortress Press, 1989).

8. The theme of God's freedom is primary in the whole program of Karl Barth. Zimmerli has brought that emphasis to fresh expression: "Prophetic proclamation thus shatters and transforms tradition in order

to announce the approach of the Living One" ("Prophetic Proclamation,"100). It is the work of liberation theologians to articulate the societal implications of this theological confession. Compare, e.g., Erhard S. Gerstenberger, "Der Befreiende Gott: Zum Standort lateinamerikanischer Theologie," in *Problems in Biblical Theology: Essays in Honor of Rolf Knierim,* ed. H. T. C. Sun et al. (Grand Rapids: Eerdmans, 1997), 145–66; José Porfirio Miranda, *Marx and the Bible: A Critique of the Philosophy of Oppression,* trans. J. Eagleson (Maryknoll, N.Y.: Orbis, 1974).

9. Marx's programmatic statement from "Critique of Hegel's Philosophy of Right," is: "Thus the criticism of heaven is transformed into the criticism of earth, the criticism of religion into the criticism of law, and the criticism of theology into the criticism of politics," quoted from Robert C. Tucker, ed., *The Marx-Engels Reader* (New York: Norton, 1972), 13.

10. James Plastaras, *The God of Exodus: The Theology of the Exodus Narratives* (Milwaukee: Bruce, 1966), chap. 3.

11. On the meaning of the term "primal scream," see Arthur Janos, *The Primal Scream* (New York: Putnam, 1970). Dorothee Soelle has shown how expressed complaint is the beginning of liberation; see *Suffering,* trans. E. R. Kalin (Philadelphia: Fortress Press, 1975).

12. Erhard Gerstenberger, "Der klagende Mensch: Anmerkungen zu den Klagegattungen in Israel," in *Probleme biblischer Theologie: Gerhard von Rad zum 70. Geburtstag,* ed. H. W. Wolff (Munich: Kaiser, 1971), 64–72. See also his important distinction between complaint and lament in "Jeremiah's Complaints," *JBL* 82 (1963): 407 n.55; his more recent *Psalms: Part 1 with an Introduction to Cultic Poetry,* FOTL 14 (Grand Rapids: Eerdmans, 1988).

13. Soelle writes that the movement from helplessness to power is accomplished through public expressions of lament, complaint, and protest (*Suffering,* 73). In describing the powerlessness that comes with failed speech, Graham Greene contrasts those who lack speech: "Most of his middle-class patients were as accustomed to spend at least ten minutes explaining a simple attack of flu. It was only in the *barrio* of the poor that he ever encountered suffering in silence, suffering which had no vocabulary to explain a degree of pain, its position or its nature"; *The Honorary Consul* (New York: Simon & Schuster, 1973), 66.

14. Hall effectively explores the theme of darkness as the arena of suffering, death, and liberty. He concludes his study: "The people of the cross, who name the darkness, can summon no absolute light, no unsul-

lied vision, whether of God or of man. It becomes for them, as for all who in the past have been grasped by his logic of the cross, a matter of faith" (*Lighten Our Darkness,* 225).

15. Characteristically the prophets do partisan theology "from below" while the royal consciousness always wants to state it "from above." See Robert McAfee Brown, "The View from Below," *A.D.* 6 (September 1977): 28–31. In that connection, the Detroit Conference on "Theology in the Americas" expressed a "hermeneutic of suspicion," a posture linked to theology from below. This phrase is identified with Paul Ricoeur, but especially in biblical studies with Elisabeth Schüssler Fiorenza, *In Memory of Her: A Feminist Theological Reconstruction of Christian Origins* (New York: Crossroad, 1983; 10th anniversary ed. 1994).

16. David Noel Freedman, "Pottery, Poetry, and Prophecy: An Essay on Biblical Poetry," *JBL* 96 (1977): 5–26; idem, "Divine Names and Titles in Early Hebrew Poetry," in *Magnalia Dei: The Mighty Acts of God. Essays on the Bible and Archaeology in Memory of G. Ernest Wright*, ed. F. M. Cross et al. (Garden City, N.Y.: Doubleday, 1976), 55–107. These two studies are reprinted in Freedman's *Pottery, Poetry, and Prophecy: Studies in Early Hebrew Poetry* (Winona Lake, Ind.: Eisenbrauns, 1980), 1–22 and 77–129.

17. On that scholarly recovery, see, for example, Phyllis Trible, "Bringing Miriam Out of the Shadows," *Bible Review* 5/1 (February 1989): 13–25.

18. Abraham Heschel, *Who Is Man?* (Stanford, Calif.: Stanford Univ. Press, 1965), chap. 6 and passim.

19. On the fundamental importance of the universe of discourse for the possibility of faith, see especially Rubem A. Alves, *Tomorrow's Child: Imagination, Creativity, and the Rebirth of Culture* (New York: Harper & Row, 1972).

Chapter 2

1. John Gager, *Kingdom and Community: The Social World of Early Christianity,* Prentice-Hall Studies in Religion Series (Englewood Cliffs, N.J.: Prentice-Hall, 1975).

2. Robert W. Friedrichs has shrewdly described the interests of sociologists and the influence of interests on scholarship in *A Sociology of Sociology* (New York: Free Press, 1970). For the paradigm we will seek to develop here, the connections are worth noting. Thus the paradigms of *system and conflict,* which Friedrichs uses for sociology, may have correlations with the royal and Mosaic traditions of Israel.

3. This particular judgment was made in a lecture given in St. Louis in 1976, but his general argument moves in this direction as well. That theological urging is not unrelated to his understanding of tribe and city. Compare Mendenhall, "Social Organization in Early Israel," in *Magnalia Dei: The Mighty Acts of God. Essays on the Bible and Archaeology in Memory of G. Ernest Wright,* ed. F. M. Cross et al. (Garden City, N.Y.: Doubleday, 1976), 132–51.

4. The term *hapiru* in various forms and with various linguistic cognates appears in the Ancient Near East in the second millennium to refer to stateless people who live at the edges of society, threaten society, and are in turn threatened by it. It is widely thought that the biblical term *Hebrew* is linked to the term; if so, then the early references to what became Israel are linked to a border social movement of marginal, precarious peoples. Recent scholarship has indicated that the term is not ethnic but is sociological and refers to those at the edge of economic and political viability in many states in the region. The theme of Hebrew-*hapiru* figures prominently in the influential sociological interpretation of Norman K. Gottwald, *The Tribes of Yahweh: A Sociology of the Religion of Liberated Israel, 1250–1050 B.C.* (Maryknoll, N.Y.: Orbis Books, 1979).

5. See George E. Mendenhall, "The Monarchy," *Interp* 29 (1975) 155–70; Frank Moore Cross, *Canaanite Myth and Hebrew Epic: Essays in the History of the Religion of Israel* (Cambridge: Harvard Univ. Press, 1973), 237–41. He refers to David's court as "rustic," a term usually assigned only to Saul. Note James Flanagan's important work, *David's Social Drama: A Hologram of Israel's Early Iron Age,* JSOTSup 73; SWBA 7 (Sheffield: JSOT, 1988).

6. Walter Brueggemann, "The Social Significance of Solomon as Patron of Wisdom," in *The Sage in Israel and the Ancient Near East,* ed. J. G. Gammie and L. G. Perdue (Winona Lake, Ind.: Eisenbrauns, 1990), 117–32.

7. The evidence is summarized by Amihai Mazar, *Archaeology of the Land of the Bible, 10,000–586 B.C.E.* (New York: Doubleday, 1992), 368–402; Gösta W. Ahlström, *The History of Ancient Palestine,* ed. D. Edelman (Minneapolis: Fortress Press, 1993), 455–542; William G. Dever, "Archaeology of the 'Age of Solomon': A Case Study in Archaeology and Historiography," in *The Age of Solomon: Scholarship at the Turn of the Millennium,* ed. L. K. Handy, Studies in the History and Culture of the Ancient Near East 11 (Leiden: Brill, 1997), 217–51.

8. Mendenhall, "The Monarchy," 160.

9. Gerhard von Rad, *Old Testament Theology,* trans. D. M. G. Stalker (New York: Harper & Brothers, 1962), 148–56. The phenomenon hypothesized by von Rad, sharply disputed by other scholars, can be read negatively as well as positively. James L. Crenshaw disputes the entire hypothesis of a Solomonic Enlightenment, whether it be viewed positively or negatively ("Introduction," in *Studies in Ancient Israelite Wisdom*, Library of Biblical Studies [New York: Ktav, 1976], 16–20).

10. See Walter Brueggemann, *In Man We Trust: The Neglected Side of Biblical Faith* (Richmond: John Knox, 1972). I believe that my interpretation in that work is essentially correct, but that it should be emphasized or read with positive interpretations surely reflects the milieu of the book, namely the theological climate of the late 1960s.

11. See the sensitive expression of distinction by Stefan Heym, *The King David Report* (New York: Putnam, 1972), 237.

12. See Walter Brueggemann, "Presence of God, Cultic," in *IDBS,* 630–33; idem, *Theology of the Old Testament: Testimony, Dispute, Advocacy* (Minneapolis: Fortress Press, 1997), 576–704, and Samuel Terrien, *The Elusive Presence: Toward a New Biblical Theology,* Religious Perspectives (New York: Harper & Row, 1978).

13. Jürgen Moltmann has seen most clearly that the loss of passion is not only a psychological factor but a predictable ingredient in social oppression; see *The Experiment Hope,* ed. and trans. M. Douglas Meeks (Philadelphia: Fortress Press, 1975), chap. 6; more extensively, idem, *The Crucified God: The Cross of Christ as the Foundation and Criticism of Christian Theology*, trans. R. A. Wilson and J. Bowden (New York: Harper & Row, 1974).

14. Thus Hans Wilhelm Hertzberg sees a direct link to the Genesis materials: "The book of Qoheleth (Ecclesiastes) was written by the author with Genesis 1–4 in front of him; Qoheleth's conceptuality is formed on the basis of creation history" (*Der Prediger,* KAT 17 [Gütersloh: Gerd Mohn, 1963], 230). Hertzberg can persuasively hypothesize that the literature is a reflection of Genesis 1–4, including the J (Yahwist) material, likely a Solomonic piece. The irony of linking this literature at least indirectly with the Solomonic situation is strengthened by the analysis of Ecclesiastes by James G. Williams, "What Does It Profit a Man?" in *Studies in Ancient Israelite Wisdom,* ed. J. L. Crenshaw (New York: Ktav, 1976), 375–89. Williams himself has no interest in that question, but the circumstance he posits for the literature is suggestive.

15. Compare Bernhard W. Anderson, *Creation Versus Chaos: The*

Reinterpretation of Mythical Symbolism in the Bible (Philadelphia: Fortress Press, 1987; reprinted with a new foreword).

16. The relation between these two strands of tradition and these two perceptions of reality is a question fundamental to current Old Testament studies. While the tradition itself argues for continuity, the scholarship reflected here not only distinguishes between them but sees deep conflict between them. Such a way of putting the question enhances the figure of Josiah, in which the two are briefly held together.

17. See Dorothee Soelle, *Suffering,* trans. E. R. Kalin (Philadelphia: Fortress Press, 1975); Moltmann, *The Experiment Hope;* Elie Wiesel in various works such as *A Beggar in Jerusalem* (New York: Schocken, 1997); Abraham Joshua Heschel, *The Prophets* (New York: Harper & Row, 1962).

18. I have used the paradigm in a quite concrete way in "A Biblical Perspective on Hunger," *ChrCent* 94 (1977), 1136–41.

19. The phrase is from Douglas John Hall, *Lighten Our Darkness: Toward an Indigenous Theology of the Cross* (Philadelphia: Westminster, 1976), chap. 3.

Chapter 3

1. Rubem A. Alves has said this most eloquently in *Tomorrow's Child: Imagination, Creativity, and the Rebirth of Culture* (New York: Harper & Row, 1972). The practice of imagination is a subversive activity not because it yields concrete acts of defiance (which it may), but because it keeps the present provisional and refuses to absolutize it. The practice of a historical imagination maintains the possibility of a future that is not continuous from the present. It is the intent of every totalitarian regime to force the future to be only an unquestioned continuation of the present.

2. As indicated in chapter 2, reference to Ecclesiastes here means no questioning of the conventional Hellenistic dating but only the observance that the cynicism of that period found a correlate in the cynicism of the Solomonic environment. Socially, the two periods are to be contrasted for Israel; but in terms of the human spirit, the two seem to come to the same sorry situation.

3. R. D. Laing, *The Politics of Experience* (New York: Pantheon, 1967), chap. 1. His programmatic statement is: "If our experience is destroyed, our behavior will be destructive" (12). The contrast between experience and behavior illuminates the recent statement of Martin Marty, *A Nation of Behavers* (Chicago: Univ. of Chicago Press, 1976). It

is the argument of this chapter that Israel's prophets must deal with this alienation between experience and behavior, that royal Israel was now only capable of behavior.

4.   Robert Jay Lifton and Eric Olson have explored the failure of symbols for death and the destructiveness of death when it lacks adequate symbolization; *Living and Dying* (New York: Praeger, 1974). Thus they speak of "psychic numbing" and a "symbolic gap" (137). They conclude that "the whole age in which we live is one of vast numbing and desensitization" caused by the technologies of death. Compare Lifton, *Death in Life: Survivors of Hiroshima* (New York: Random House, 1967), 474, "Technology Leads to Disconnected Death"; idem, *History and Human Survival: Essays on the Young and Old, Survivors and the Dead, Peace and War, and on Contemporary Psychohistory* (New York: Random House, 1970), 175, in which Lifton speaks of death without symbols as "severance of the sense of connection." The prophet's stance over against the king nurtures adequate symbolization and therefore insists upon connectedness.

5.   Effective symbols are those that have grown out of the history of the community. Thus we are speaking not of universal myths but of symbolization appropriate to a peculiar history. In Israel we may then refer to the memories of incongruity that serve Israel through the prophecy of Jeremiah. See the provocative statement of Peter R. Ackroyd, "Continuity and Discontinuity: Rehabilitation and Authentication," in *Tradition and Theology in the Old Testament,* ed. D. A. Knight (Philadelphia: Fortress Press, 1977), 215–34. There is a danger in symbols that provide continuity, for they may lessen the reality of the discontinuity; but Ackroyd has stated for Israel that which Lifton sees in terms of our own culture.

6.   The anguish and passion that make such speech authoritative cannot be in terms of comprehensive myths but must be out of the experience of the community. Thus the study of the language of metaphor and parable is to let Israel experience its own experience, as Laing has seen. On the concreteness of language, see Sallie McFague TeSelle, *Speaking in Parables: A Study in Metaphor and Theology* (Philadelphia: Fortress Press, 1975); John Dominic Crossan, *The Dark Interval: Towards a Theology of Story* (Sonoma, Calif.: Polebridge, 1988; reprint ed.); William R. Herzog II, *Parables as Subversive Speech: Jesus as Pedagogue of the Oppressed* (Louisville: Westminster John Knox, 1994). It is the task of the prophet to energize the metaphors resulting from historical experience.

7. On a quite different critical judgment of this text, see George E. Mendenhall, "The Shady Side of Wisdom: The Date and Purpose of Genesis 3," in *A Light Unto My Path: Old Testament Studies in Honor of Jacob M. Myers*, ed. H. N. Bream et al. (Philadelphia: Temple Univ. Press, 1974), 319–34. The dating to the exile as Mendenhall proposes, vis à vis conventional Solomonic dating, may suggest important parallels between the two periods.

8. Thus apathy and official optimism have ideological purposes. Against that, grief and lamentation, as urged and practiced by the prophets, begin the dismantling of royal reality. Expressed suffering is the beginning of counterpower. See G. Müller-Fahrenholz, "Overcoming Apathy," *EcRev* 27 (1975) 48–56. He follows the study of A. Mitscherlich in noting the inability of Germans to grieve over the Nazi period. Such an observation coincides with the findings of Lifton. The argument of Müller-Fahrenholz agrees with the point made here, that without grief there will not be the overcoming of apathy and the embrace of new tasks. On pathos as a prerequisite for protest, see James L. Crenshaw, "The Human Dilemma and Literature of Dissent," in *Tradition and Theology in the Old Testament,* 235–37; Walter Brueggemann, "A Shape for Old Testament Theology, II: Embrace of Pain," *CBQ* 47 (1985): 395–415.

9. Compare William L. Holladay, "The Background of Jeremiah's Self-Understanding: Moses, Samuel, and Psalm 22," *JBL* 83 (1964): 153–64. Less directly, see Sheldon Blank, "The Prophet as Paradigm," in *Essays in Old Testament Ethics: J. Philip Hyatt, in Memoriam*, ed. J. L. Crenshaw and J. T. Willis (New York: Ktav, 1974), 111–30. On grief as definitional for the tradition of Jeremiah, see Peter Weter, "Leiden und Leidenerfahung im Buch Jeremia," *ZTK* 74 (1977): 123–50.

10. On the Lord's passion borne by Jeremiah, see Abraham Joshua Heschel, *The Prophets* (New York: Harper & Row, 1962), chap. 6.

11. Compare Karl Barth, *Church Dogmatics* I/2, trans. G. W. Bromiley (Edinburgh: T. & T. Clark, 1956), sec. 14. Much of his argument concerns the freedom of God and the royal penchant to deny time for some "eternal now." Against that, biblical faith lives in God's times, times of recollection and expectation.

12. On Jeremiah's remarkable use of this metaphor, see the statement of James Muilenburg, "The Terminology of Adversity in Jeremiah," in *Translating and Understanding the Old Testament: Essays in Honor of Herbert Gordon May*, ed. H. T. Frank and W. L. Reed (New York: Abingdon, 1970), 42–63.

13. See the delicate interpretation of Phyllis Trible, "The Gift of the Poem: A Rhetorical Study of Jeremiah 31:15-22," *Andover Newton Quarterly* 17 (1977), 271–80; idem, *God and the Rhetoric of Sexuality*, OBT (Philadelphia: Fortress Press, 1978). See also Walter Brueggemann, "Texts That Linger, Words That Explode," in *Texts That Linger, Words That Explode* (Minneapolis: Fortress Press, 1999), 1–19, esp. 4–7.

14. Terence E. Fretheim, *The Suffering of God: An Old Testament Perspective,* OBT (Philadelphia: Fortress Press, 1984), 132–36.

15. Most poignant is the presentation of the Lord by Elie Wiesel, *Ani Maamin: A Song Lost and Found Again* (New York: Random House, 1973).

16. Douglas John Hall has related the negativity theme both to the theology of the cross and to our social situation; *Lighten Our Darkness: Toward an Indigenous Theology of the Cross* (Philadelphia: Westminster, 1976), especially chap. 2.

Chapter 4

1. Thomas M. Raitt, *A Theology of Exile: Judgment/Deliverance in Jeremiah and Ezekiel* (Philadelphia: Fortress Press, 1977).

2. John Bright, *Jeremiah*, AB 21 (Garden City, N.Y.: Doubleday, 1965). For different perspectives, see Walter Brueggemann, *A Commentary on Jeremiah: Exile/Homecoming* (Grand Rapids: Eerdmans, 1998), and Robert P. Carroll, *Jeremiah: A Commentary,* OTL (Philadelphia: Westminster, 1986).

3. See John Kautsky, *The Politics of Aristocratic Empires* (Chapel Hill: Univ. of North Carolina Press, 1982), 7–8; K. C. Hanson and Douglas E. Oakman, *Palestine in the Time of Jesus: Social Structures and Social Conflicts* (Minneapolis: Fortress Press, 1998) 64–70.

4. Norman K. Gottwald, *Studies in the Book of Lamentations,* SBT 1/14 (2d ed. Chicago: Allenson, 1962).

5. Bernhard W. Anderson has explored two quite distinct dimensions of the tradition to which appeal is made; but in each case it is to a specific Israelite tradition. See "Exodus Typology in Second Isaiah," in *Israel's Prophetic Heritage: Essays in Honor of James Muilenburg,* ed. B. W. Anderson and W. Harrelson (New York: Harper & Brothers, 1962), 177–95; "Exodus and Covenant in Second Isaiah and Prophetic Tradition," in *Magnalia Dei: The Mighty Acts of God. Essays on the Bible and Archaeology in Memory of G. Ernest Wright*, ed. F. M. Cross et al. (Garden City, N.Y.: Doubleday, 1976), 339–60.

6. Prophetic ministry must see more clearly than we have in recent time the integral connection between speech and hope! It is only speech

that makes hope possible, and when the royal consciousness of technology stops serious speech, it precludes hope. This was seen clearly by Paul in his claim in Rom 10:14-21.

7. On the subversive power of hope as a way of dismantling, see John M. Swomley Jr., *Liberation Ethics* (New York: Macmillan, 1972).

8. The richness of the language of Second Isaiah suggests that the poet not only lived in but knew and utilized the literature of his own time; compare especially Klaus Baltzer, *Deutero-Isaiah,* trans. M. Kohl, Hermeneia (Minneapolis: Fortress Press, 2001). The links between Job and Second Isaiah on creation theology have been noted by Robert Pfeiffer, "Dual Origin of Hebrew Monotheism," *JBL* 46 (1927): 193–206. The possibility that Second Isaiah is a response to the chagrin of Lamentations is worth pursuing. See below, that the poetry of Second Isaiah begins with "Comfort, comfort" (Isa 40:1) is probably a response to the "none to comfort" of Lamentations (1:2, 17).

9. The reference is only a partially facetious one to June Bingham's biography of Reinhold Niebuhr, *Courage to Change: An Introduction to the Life and Thought of Reinhold Niebuhr* (New York: Scribner, 1961). That same phrase is not only applicable to the Lord of Israel but is an important prophetic assertion against the immutability of God fostered by the royal consciousness that yearns for eternal stability.

10. Raitt, *A Theology of Exile,* 188–89.

11. Such waiting is of course not passivity. See the recent hints by Dorothee Soelle, *Revolutionary Patience,* trans. Rita Kimber and Robert Kimber (Maryknoll, N.Y.: Orbis, 1977), and the older statement by Christoph Blumhardt under the phrase "Warten und Eilen!" Concerning the dialectic of action and waiting in the Blumhardts, see Karl Barth's comments in the afterword to Christoph Blumhardt's *Action in Waiting* (Farmington, Pa.: Plough, 1998).

Chapter 5

1. That same contrast and alternative between powerful king and new claimant is presented in the present shape of Jeremiah 34–35. In their present form, the two narratives are surely juxtaposed intentionally. In Jeremiah 34, the calculating holders of the land (not unlike Herod) play a deathly game with land and freedom, and in the end they are sentenced to death, for their calculating game cannot succeed. By contrast, in chap. 35 the Rechabites—those who claim nothing and who have nothing, except a determination to obedience—end with a bless-

ing. The Nazarene identity of Jesus and the lifestyle of the Rechabites suggest a more than casual parallel.

2. See the perceptive statement about Lucan summaries by Paul S. Minear, *To Heal and to Reveal: The Prophetic Vocation According to Luke* (New York: Seabury, 1976), 63–77. The Magnificat is seen as one of several texts that present, Luke as a theology of the necessity of the impossible. Other texts shaped in parallel fashion, according to Minear, are: 4:18-19; 6:20-22; 7:22; and 14:21.

3. See Minear, *To Heal,* 63–65 on the theme of inversion represented in this most characteristic text of Luke. The hope carried in the passage is an appeal to the spirit, "to heaven," i.e., to that which the present order cannot administer.

4. Hannah Arendt, *The Human Condition* (Chicago: Univ. of Chicago Press, 1958), 236–43: "The discoverer of the role of forgiveness in the realm of human affairs was Jesus of Nazareth" (238). "It is his insistence on the 'power to forgive' even more than his performance of miracles, that shocks the people" (239 n. 76).

5. On the Sabbath as a sign of the freedom of the messianic age, see Jürgen Moltmann, *The Church in the Power of the Spirit: A Contribution of Messianic Ecclesiology,* trans. M. Kohl (Minneapolis: Fortress Press, 1993), 261–78. Moltmann quotes Fromm to good advantage: "Death is suspended and life rules on the Sabbath day" (270). Compare Hans Walter Wolff, *Anthropology of the Old Testament,* trans. M. Kohl (Philadelphia: Fortress Press, 1974), 135–42, on the radical social implications of the day. See also Abraham Joshua Heschel, *The Sabbath: Its Meaning for Modern Man* (New York: Farrar, Straus and Young, 1951).

6. Paul W. Hollenbach, "Jesus, Demoniacs, and Public Authorities: A Socio-Historical Study," *JAAR* 49 (1981): 567–88; John J. Pilch, *Healing in the New Testament: Insights from Medical and Mediterranean Anthropology* (Minneapolis: Fortress Press, 2000); Norman K. Gottwald, "The Plot Structure of Marvel or Problem Resolution Stories in the Elijah-Elisha Narratives and Some Musings on Sitz im Leben," in idem, *The Hebrew Bible in Its Social World and in Ours* (Atlanta: Scholars, 1993), 119–30.

7. Elisabeth Schüssler Fiorenza, *In Memory of Her: A Feminist Reconstruction of Christian Origins* (New York: Crossroad, 1983; 10th anniversary ed., 1994); Kathleen Corley, *Private Women, Public Meals: Social Conflict in the Synoptic Tradition* (Peabody, Mass.: Hendrickson, 1993); Ekkehard W. Stegemann and Wolfgang Stegemann, *The Jesus Movement: A Social History of Its First Century* (Minneapolis: Fortress Press, 1998), 378–88.

8. Douglas E. Oakman, "Jesus and Agrarian Palestine: The Factor of Debt," in *SBL Seminar Papers 1985* (Atlanta: Scholars, 1985), 57–73; K. C. Hanson and Douglas E. Oakman, *Palestine in the Time of Jesus: Social Structures and Social Conflicts* (Minneapolis: Fortress Press, 1998), 119–20, 152–53.

9. K. C. Hanson, "Sin, Purification, and Group Process," in *Problems in Biblical Theology: Essays in Honor of Rolf Knierim,* ed. H. T. C. Sun et al. (Grand Rapids: Eerdmans, 1997), 167–91; this article deals with Leviticus 4–5; Jeremiah 7–8 and 26; Acts 2.

10. There can be little doubt that, in his temple sermon of Jeremiah 7, Jeremiah had to combat a high theology of Jerusalem in part encouraged by Isaiah. The critique of the claims of Jerusalem inevitably meant conflict with the royal consciousness. On the royal dimension of the Jerusalem tradition, see John H. Hayes, "The Traditions of Zion's Inviolability," *JBL* 82 (1963): 419–26; J. J. M. Roberts, "The Davidic Origin of the Zion Tradition," *JBL* 92 (1973): 329–44; idem, "Zion in the Theology of the Davidic-Solomonic Empire," in *Studies in the Period of David and Solomon and Other Essays*, ed. T. Ishida (Winona Lake, Ind.: Eisenbrauns, 1982), 93–108; Jon D. Levenson, "Zion Traditions," in *ABD* 6:1098–102.

11. On the law and social convention as related to biblical faith, see the critique by José Porfirio Miranda, *Marx and the Bible: A Critique of the Philosophy of Oppression,* trans. J. Eagleson (Maryknoll, N.Y.: Orbis, 1974), especially chap. 4.

12. José Porfirio Miranda argues in a similar direction concerning compassion, though with reference to a different Greek term; *Being and the Messiah: The Message of St. John,* trans. J. Eagleson (Maryknoll, N.Y.: Orbis, 1977), 148–53.

13. Both the value and the deficiency on structural criticism are evident in the various discussions of the parable of the good Samaritan in *Semeia* 2 (1974).

14. That claim is of course at the center of prophetic faith and of liberation theology. A somewhat different rendering of the same reality is expressed by Paul Elmem in commenting on the poet Robert Lowell: ". . . the secret known to poets and to nightingales; that pain can be managed when it finds a perfect expression" ("Death of an Elfking," *ChrCent* 94 [1977], 10–57). That is the secret completely denied to the managers who shape the empire.

15. It now is clear that the "woe oracle" used by the prophets and then by Jesus is to be understood not as a harsh renunciation but as a

summons to grieve a death. Compare W. Eugene March, "Prophecy," in *Old Testament Form Criticism,* ed. J. H. Hayes, TUMSR 2 (San Antonio: Trinity Univ. Press, 1974), 164–65, and references there to the works of Richard J. Clifford, Erhard Gerstenberger, Günther Wanke, and James G. Williams. The recharacterization of the form in that way is indicative of a quite new discernment of what the prophets are about. Such a form indicates grief as the proper context for such speech and indicates the heavy misunderstanding of the prophets in many circles where "woe" is understood as threat and rage. For an interpretation of "woe" in terms of honor and shame, see K. C. Hanson, "How Honorable! How Shameful! A Cultural Analysis of Matthew's Makarisms and Reproaches," *Semeia* 68 (1996): 81–111.

16. The cross thus is the announcement that God has abandoned all theology of triumph and glory. See the arguments of Douglas John Hall, *Lighten Our Darkness: Toward an Indigenous Theology of the Cross* (Philadelphia: Westminster, 1976).

17. Paul Lehmann, *The Transformation of Politics* (New York: Harper & Row, 1975) 48–70.

18. Terence E. Fretheim, *The Suffering of God: An Old Testament Perspective,* OBT (Philadelphia: Fortress Press, 1984), 132–36.

19. The argument of Lifton from chap. 3 is pertinent here. The collapse has to do finally not with visible, imperial items but with the collapse of the symbol system. Alienation from a symbol system that leaves us disconnected is the harshness of this criticism.

20. See R. H. Fuller, *The Foundations of New Testament Christology* (New York: Scribner, 1965), 207.

21. On embrace of negation see Douglas John Hall, *Lighten Our Darkness: Toward an Indigenous Theology of the Cross* (Philadelphia: Westminster, 1976), chap. 2 and passim. See also Walter Brueggemann, "A Shape for Old Testament Theology, II: The Embrace of Pain," *CBQ* 47 (1985): 395–415.

Chapter 6

1. On the distinction between hope and process or optimism, see Douglas John Hall, *Lighten Our Darkness: Toward an Indigenous Theology of the Cross* (Philadelphia: Westminster, 1976), chaps. 1 and 3; also Jürgen Moltmann, *Theology of Hope: On the Ground and the Implications of a Christian Eschatology,* trans. J. W. Leitch (New York: Harper & Row, 1967), chap. 2.

2. The census stands in Israel for the ability of the royal apparatus to regiment people against freedom and justice; thus it evokes curse (2 Samuel 24). Perhaps with intuitive correctness, the Chronicler has credited the policy to Satan (1 Chronicles 21). There is indeed something satanic about such an exercise of control. Frank Moore Cross links the census to the entire development of royal ideology (*Canaanite Myth and Hebrew Epic: Essays on the History of the Religion of Israel* [Cambridge: Harvard Univ. Press, 1973], 227–40). It is not difficult to see why it was later discerned as satanic. Thus the discernment of Satan as having socioeconomic dimensions. Walter Brueggemann, "2 Samuel 21–24: An Appendix of Deconstruction?" *CBQ* 50 (1988): 383–97; idem, *First and Second Samuel*, Interpretation (Atlanta: John Knox, 1990), 350–57; K. C. Hanson, "When the King Crosses the Line: Royal Deviance and Restitution in Levantine Ideologies," *BTB* 26 (1996): 11–25.

3. On the restoration of language as the first act of hope, see Dorothee Soelle, *Suffering,* trans. E. R. Kalin (Philadelphia: Fortress Press, 1975).

4. John J. Pilch, "Selecting an Appropriate Model: Leprosy—A Test Case," in *Healing in the New Testament: Insights from Medical and Mediterranean Anthropology* (Minneapolis: Fortress Press, 2000), 39–54; Jerome H. Neyrey, "Clean/Unclean, Pure/Polluted, and Holy/Profane: The Idea and the System of Purity," in *The Social Sciences and New Testament Interpretation,* ed. R. L. Rohrbaugh (Peabody, Mass.: Hendrickson, 1996), 80–104.

5. In commenting on the Beatitudes, José Porfirio Miranda observes the socioeconomic dimension to the blessing: "I wonder where there is more faith and hope: in believing 'in the God who raises the dead' (Rom 4:17) or in believing like Luke in the God who 'filled the hungry with good things and sent the rich away empty' (Luke 1:53)?" (*Marx and the Bible: A Critique of the Philosophy of Oppression,* trans. J. Eagleson [Maryknoll, N.Y.: Orbis, 1974], 217).

6. On the claims of the Beatitudes, see Jürgen Moltmann, *The Church in the Power of the Spirit: A Contribution of Messianic Ecclesiology,* trans. M. Kohl (Minneapolis: Fortress Press, 1993), 80–81. He concludes that the "people of the Beatitudes" must be converted to the future. On the Beatitudes in general, see: Michael Crosby, *The Spirituality of the Beatitudes: Matthew's Challenge for First World Christians* (Maryknoll, N.Y.: Orbis, 1981); Hans Dieter Betz, "The Beatitudes of the Sermon on the Mount (Matt. 5:3-12): Observations on Their Literary Form and Theological Significance," in idem, *Essays on the Sermon on the Mount,*

trans. L. L. Welborn (Philadelphia: Fortress Press, 1985) ,17–36; idem, *The Sermon on the Mount,* Hermeneia (Minneapolis: Fortress Press, 1994); K. C. Hanson, "How Honorable! How Shameful! A Cultural Interpretation of Matthew's Makarisms and Reproaches," *Semeia* 68 (1996): 81–111.

Chapter 7

1. At the level of individual personality, this is the argument of George Benson, *Then Joy Breaks Through* (New York: Seabury, 1972). He begins his last chapter in this way: "The transformation of all time and the Christian prototype of joy is the resurrection of Christ" (123). His entire book is about the meaning of the cross on the way to life.

2. In a way that is enormously helpful and a bit deductive, I have been helped greatly by the research of Elizabeth Kübler-Ross, *On Death and Dying* (New York: Macmillan, 1969). See my discussion of her paradigm in relation to the faith of Israel in "The Formfulness of Grief," *Interp* 31 (1977): 263–75. See also idem, "Psalms of Disorientation," in *The Message of the Psalms: A Theological Commentary* (Minneapolis: Fortress Press, 1984), 50–121.

Postscript

1. Andrew McAuley Smith, "Prophets in the Pews: Testing Walter Brueggemann's Thesis in *The Prophetic Imagination* in the Practice of Ministry" (D.Min. thesis, Princeton Seminary, 1999).

2. Ibid., 49–86.

3. Ibid., 92.

4. Ibid., 120.

In Retrospect (PI at Forty)

1. Robert Jay Lifton, *Witness to an Extreme Century: A Memoir* (New York: Free Press, 2011). On pages 67–68 and 381 Lifton outlines the recurring "deadly sins" of totalism.

2. Emmanuel Levinas, *Totality and Infinity: An Essay on Exteriority* (Pittsburgh, PA: Duquesne University Press, 1969).

3. William T. Cavanaugh, *Torture and Eucharist* (Oxford: Blackwell, 1998) has traced out the contest of imaginations in Chile under the Pinochet regime. "Social imagination is not a mere representation of something more real; it is not some ideological 'superstructure'

which reflects the material 'base.' . . . The imagination of a society is the condition of possibility for the organization and signification of bodies in a society. The imagination is the drama in which bodies are invested. . . . If torture is the imagination of the state, the Eucharist is the imagination of the church" (57, 229). Cavanaugh quotes from a novel of Lawrence Thornton: "We have to believe in the power of imagination because it is all we have, and ours is stronger than theirs" (279). Cavanaugh concludes: "To participate in the Eucharist is to live inside God's imagination" (279).

It is clear that in ancient Israel the imagination of the royal-priestly-scribal establishment in Jerusalem was very powerful; the prophets sought to out-imagine that enterprise. So among us, the imagination of market ideology (relentlessly offered in the liturgies of mindless televisions and most poignantly through the NFL as a festival of money, sex, and violence) is a powerful form of imagination; the prophetic task, now as then, is to out-imagine that enterprise.

4. *Hopeful Imagination: Prophetic Voices in Exile* (Philadelphia: Fortress Press, 1986); *Reality, Grief, Hope: Three Urgent Prophetic Tasks* (Grand Rapids: Eerdmans, 2014); *The Practice of Prophetic Imagination: Preaching an Emancipatory Word* (Minneapolis: Fortress Press, 2012).

5. "The Costly Loss of Lament," *JSOT* 11/36 (1986): 57–71.

6. Douglas John Hall, *Lighten Our Darkness: Toward an Indigenous Theology of the Cross* (Philadelphia: Westminster, 1976) has provided a reliable compelling exposition of the Theology of the Cross.

7. "The Liturgy of Abundance, the Myth of Scarcity," *The Christian Century* 116/10 (March 24–31, 1999): 342–47.

8. On market ideology, see most poignantly Gerald Berthoud, "Market," in *The Development Dictionary: A Guide to Knowledge as Power*, ed. Wolfgang Sachs, 2nd ed. (New York: Zed, 2010), 74–94. Berthoud makes clear that "the market" has morphed from a matrix for trade to a regulatory principle that intends to impose its categories on all of our common life.

Selected Bibliography

Birch, Bruce C. *Let Justice Roll Down: The Old Testament, Ethics, and Christian Life.* Louisville: Westminster John Knox, 1991. [Note: Chapter 6: "Royal Ideal and Royal Reality," 198–239.]

Blenkinsopp, Joseph. *A History of Prophecy in Israel.* Rev. ed. Louisville: Westminster John Knox, 1996.

Chaney, Marvin L. "Systemic Study of the Israelite Monarchy." *Semeia* 37 (1986): 53–76.

Coats, George W. "The King's Loyal Opposition: Obedience and Authority in Exodus 32–34." In *Canon and Authority: Essays in Old Testament Religion and Theology,* edited by G. W. Coats and B. O. Long, 91–109. Philadelphia: Fortress Press, 1977. [Note: this deals with both Moses and Jeremiah]

Gordon, Robert P., ed. *The Place Is Too Small for Us: The Israelite Prophets in Recent Scholarship,* SBTS 5. Winona Lake, Ind.: Eisenbrauns, 1995.

Gottwald, Norman K. "The Biblical Prophetic Critique of Political Economy: Its Ground and Import." In *God and Capitalism: A Prophetic Critique of Market Economy,* edited by J. M. Thomas and V. Visick, 11–29. Madison, Wis.: A-R Editions, 1991. Reprinted in Norman K. Gottwald, *The Hebrew Bible in Its Social World and in Ours,* Semeia Studies, 349–64. Atlanta: Scholars, 1993.

―――. "A Hypothesis about Social Class in Monarchic Israel in the Light of Contemporary Studies of Social Class and Stratification." In idem, *The Hebrew Bible in Its Social World and in Ours*, Semeia Studies, 139–64. Atlanta: Scholars, 1993.

————. "Social Class as an Analytic and Hermeneutical Category in Biblical Studies." *JBL* 112 (1993): 3–22.

Handy, Lowell K., ed. *The Age of Solomon: Scholarship at the Turn of the Millennium*. Studies in the History and Culture of the Ancient Near East 11. Leiden: Brill, 1997. [24 articles]

Holladay, William L. *Jeremiah*. Vol. 1. Hermeneia. Philadelphia: Fortress Press, 1986.

————. *Jeremiah*. Vol. 2. Hermeneia. Minneapolis: Fortress Press, 1989.

Hutton, Rodney R. *Charisma and Authority in Israelite Society*. Minneapolis: Fortress Press, 1994. [Especially chaps. 1, 2, 5]

Ishida, Tomoo, ed. *Studies in the Period of David and Solomon and Other Essays*. Winona Lake, Ind.: Eisenbrauns, 1982.

Koch, Klaus. "The Language of Prophecy: Thoughts on the Macrosyntax of the *debar YHWH* and Its Semantic Implications in the Deuteronomistic History." In *Problems in Biblical Theology: Essays in Honor of Rolf Knierim,* edited by H. T. C. Sun et al., 210–21. Grand Rapids: Eerdmans, 1997.

Overholt, Thomas W. *Channels of Prophecy: The Social Dynamics of Prophetic Activity*. Minneapolis: Fortress Press, 1989.

Smith, Daniel L. *The Religion of the Landless: The Social Context of the Babylonian Exile*. Bloomington, Ind.: Meyer-Stone, 1989.

Whitelam, Keith W. "Israelite Kingship: The Royal Ideology and Its Opponents." In *The World of Ancient Israel: Sociological, Anthropological and Political Perspectives,* edited by R. E. Clements, 119–39. Cambridge: Cambridge Univ. Press, 1989.

Whitelam, Keith W. "The Symbols of Power: Aspects of Royal Propaganda in the United Monarchy." *BA* 49 (1986): 166–73.

Wilson, Robert R. *Prophecy and Society in Ancient Israel*. Philadelphia: Fortress Press, 1980.

Scripture Index